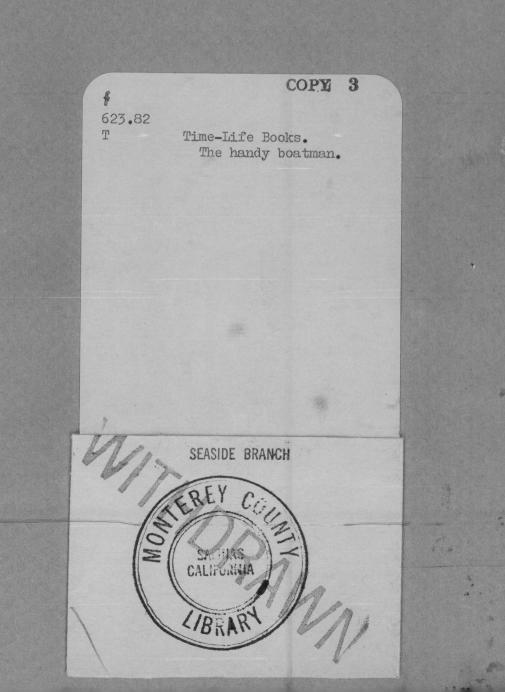

The Handy Boatman

The Handy Boatman

By the Editors of
TIME-LIFE BOOKS

The
TIME-LIFE Library of Boating

TIME-LIFE BOOKS, NEW YORK

The Satisfaction of Making Things Better

The Satisfaction of Making Things Better

by David M. Parker

I have never known a boatman who could look at a yacht—his own or some-one else's, a new one or an old one—without finding something that could be done to improve it. One reason is individual taste; another is that all boat-men seem to be devout tinkerers. A new boat often comes from the produc-tion line bearing only those fittings required by common sense—or by the law for safety's sake—leaving the new owner an almost blank slate on which to express his creativity. A used boat, though in all likelihood it will have been modified and re-equipped since it left the production line, tempts the new owner to correct the "mistakes" of the former owner.

With one owner these corrections may involve stripping a boat of gadgets and fillips, until it takes on the air of Bristol-fashion tidiness, or even a bare starkness reminiscent of a man-of-war's forepeak. With another it may mean affixing every conceivable form of electronic and carpenterial gadgetry in every available space. Yet another owner may have a passion for traditional décor, and line his cabins with white-painted panels framed in varnished ma-hogany and hung with brass kerosene lamps. My own tastes are impulsive, eclectic and variable. Hence my boat seems always to be in a state of last-minute finishing (or imminent collapse) as a locker here, a fitting there, a gal-ley or a bunk is summarily yanked out to be either modernized or redesigned. In fact, most of my boating life has been a constant ripping out and modi-fying process, sometimes done too hastily and sometimes with hilarious or disastrous consequences.

Beyond the eternal yen for tinkering, there are plenty of good reasons for modifying boats. For example, a boat can be made much safer than it was be-fore by the installation of smoke and fume detectors, bilge-water alarms and the like. A pressure water system with a heater makes living aboard more com-fortable. A good grating on the cockpit sole keeps feet drier, and helps re-duce the chance of a midnight overboard drill when the wind is blowing hard offshore. A fine paneling job below and some better-than-routine woodwork here and there enhance the vessel's looks and resale value. By doing the work yourself you will incur fewer expenses than if you hired the work out, and as an important dividend, you will learn your boat's inner workings and idio-syncrasies. In spite of some inevitable errors, the jobs you do yourself are more likely to get done the way you want them done. And for me, one of the most rewarding aspects of handiwork is the pride I take in saying I did it my-self. Finally, since you can't sail all the time, what better way to spend some happy, productive hours than in improving your boat?

There are a few jobs that I would not recommend for the novice. Be wary of modifications that might affect the stability of the vessel: don't install a large extra tank up under the decks or attempt to put a massive deck locker high up in a small boat without calling in a naval architect first—such am-bitious projects carry a lot of weight and can alter the trim of the boat. Be equally wary of alterations that will substantially influence the boat's per-formance, e.g., a change in the position of the mast or the rudder; these are both critical jobs that require the skill, knowledge and judgment of the yacht designer or the professional shipwright.

There are some other cautions that I would impress on first-time boat car-penters. Measure your desires against your skills and start with projects that will develop your talents gradually—while still making noticeable improve-ments in the comfort and convenience of your boat. Before tackling a cock-pit grating, which can be expensive if it is not right, try a few add-on things like a navigator's rack or a locker shelf that, if done wrong, can easily be put right with no real damage either to your pocketbook or to the boat. Then you might work up to installing a Dorade vent over the galley or a mushroom vent over the head compartment. The improvement that such installations make

Expert handyman David M. Parker takes a breather on the bow of Dawn Treader II, a 42-foot cutter that, with the assistance of his wife, he built and altered and fiddled with and improved, from keel shoe to mast cap.

in the quality of life aboard is well-nigh miraculous. But for all that, even these are astonishingly simple to do once you have become a bit used to working with tools aboard ship.

Another word of advice: limit yourself at first to short-term projects that do not immobilize you and the boat for long periods of time. In my early boating days I once saw a minor flaw in my boat and in a flurry of excess zeal tore off the cabin and removed most of the interior joinery before reason returned. It took three months before the boat was ready to sail again.

As you develop experience in the art of modification you will gain confidence. You will make your share of mistakes, of course, but the mark of the good handyman is not how few mistakes he makes, but how well he can recoup from the mistakes he does make. I once made a perfectly splendid paper pattern for a galley countertop. It was very intricate, for there were many ribs to be fitted around and cutouts for sink and faucets to be made. Having satisfied myself that the fit and layout were perfect, I took the pattern home and traced the outlines on a fine piece of teak plywood. I carefully cut out the piece with a high-speed router to avoid splintering the wood. Then I took it down to the boat—and found to my dismay that I had reversed the pattern when laying it on the wood, and so the carefully cut wood was useless for a countertop. I did manage to salvage part of the reversed countertop for a new lockertop—but I will never again fail to mark one side of a pattern with the word "top."

I have also learned since then to work out a number of alterations on paper before I start sawing up expensive wood or removing existing structures in the boat itself. When setting out to make any extensive changes I always draw the outlines of the boat to scale. I then cut out cardboard outlines of bunks, stoves, winches, toilets and other furnishings, and then shuffle them around on the drawing until the best arrangement shows itself. I don't know how many boatmen have installed hanging lockers for foul-weather gear, only to find they have made it inconvenient for themselves and their passengers to get in and out of the cabin—or how many have put in winches without thinking about the fact that every winch needs surrounding elbow room for whoever cranks the handle. Laying out things first to scale can prevent such blunders; it also prevents the infuriatingly useless expenditure of time and money that blunders entail.

There are some other things to think about in advance. Build everything that you put aboard as though you intended it to last a hundred years—despite the odds that you will later want to alter it. Handrails, for instance, should be through-bolted and made of stout material. They must be able to withstand the weight of the heaviest-conceivable crew member making his way past the cabin in the roughest weather at sea. If in doubt concerning the installation of any equipment, read the manufacturer's instructions carefully; then set the equipment temporarily in place (with tape if necessary) to see if you can operate it satisfactorily. Most important, ask a genuine expert. Most expert boat fiddlers are eager to crow about their own successes and will give you more advice than you can handle.

In fact, after a few successful go-rounds you may soon succumb to this syndrome yourself, for there are few temptations to which boatmen submit more readily than displaying the results of their own skill and ingenuity. Years ago, in an old vessel named *Laguna*, one of the many yachts I have owned and fiddled with, I built a quite marvelous table that folded up from a bulkhead. It locked in place when not in use and had a folding, spring-mounted leg that snapped into place when lowered. Above it, folding down from the same bulkhead, was a combination chart table and rack. Since the cabin was quite cramped, and since I detest using the dining table as a chart table, the arrangement was a marvelous space-saver. I have long since sold *Laguna*, but the memory of my table arrangement is still fresh and bright. In fact, now that I think of it, I just may do the same thing aboard my new boat—as soon as I finish installing an onyx countertop in the head.

1 The most obvious and often the most useful place to start making improvements on a boat is abovedecks. There the boatman is working in good light and generally in open space with plenty of elbowroom. Moreover, the majority of topside modifications require straightforward carpentry skills with which most modern boatmen—in fact, most householders—are familiar. Finally, with deckside improvements, there is the double bonus of having not only a better boat but, by the application of a little craftsmanship, a conspicuously better-looking boat. Despite their basic simplicity, however, not long ago many of the modifications shown and explained on the subsequent pages would have been within the ca-

CUSTOM PROJECTS TOPSIDE

pabilities of only a few accomplished—and mainly professional—marine craftsmen. But with the proliferation in many home workshops of reliable, relatively inexpensive power tools, such as electric drills, saber saws, orbital sanders and the like, difficult bits of handwork become mechanized and simple. In addition, the specialized tools the boatman will occasionally require —a plug cutter, for instance, or a doweling jig—can be purchased at reasonable cost. Other tools, such as a belt sander or a band saw, can usually be rented or borrowed.

Besides having a handshaking acquaintance with such tools, the boatman needs at least a modest understanding of the special demands of marine carpentry. Putting in a simple plywood shelf, as described on pages 20-21, will mean reproducing exactly some of the complex curves and odd angles that abound in boats. Rough sketches, more complete working drawings, and sometimes templates made of wood, cardboard or heavy paper can be indispensable guides, especially when a project is started in a workshop for later mounting aboard.

The boatman must keep in mind, too, that the sea never relents and it cannot be fooled. Thus the various materials that are to be employed for marine carpentry must be strong, durable and water resistant. For example, certain woods are uniquely suited to an aquatic environment. Teak, for instance, is iron-hard and its natural oil makes it particularly resistant to weathering. Its principal function aboard boats is for decking, but it is also excellent for cockpit gratings like the one shown at left, deck lockers, swim platforms and other heavy-duty uses. Honduras mahogany, which is almost as hard as teak yet is less expensive and easier to work with, does especially well for grab rails. Versatile plywood serves for everything from locker shelves to doublers—the backup plates that are vital to the installation of through-hull fittings, especially on fiberglass boats. But only marine-grade plywood, laminated with waterproof glue, will do.

Metal fastenings must be noncorroding. Shiny stainless steel or Monel look best where screwheads, bolts and nuts are exposed to view. Elsewhere, the marine bronze alloys are more than adequate. In order to avoid the corrosion that results from combining unlike metals in a damp and salty atmosphere, the boatman should be careful to install steel fastenings with steel fittings, bronze with bronze, etc.

All through-hull installations should be sealed with a marine bedding compound. When bolting an outboard-motor bracket to a fiberglass transom, for example, the boatman should use a compound that adheres to fiberglass and that retains some elasticity, since the installation is subject to considerable vibration. Resorcinol or any other waterproof glue is best for all wood joints that are glued. When the glue is applied, it should be spread thin with a putty knife, and the joints must be fashioned with sufficient care so that wood meets wood at all points.

The boatman at left works at his tool bench ashore to join a side piece of framing to a teak grid. When the grid is complete, he will fit it onto his cockpit sole.

Room for Improvements

There is plenty of room for the improvement of abovedecks equipment on almost any boat, large or small, power or sail. Shown in blue here and on pages 14-15 —and explained on subsequent pages —are 10 modifications, pictured in the positions they might occupy when installed on a typical powerboat or sailboat. A few of the projects, like the swim platform below, are designed for powerboats, while the Dorade vent on page 15 is best suited for a sailboat. The rest can be adapted for virtually any type of craft. And all the projects are within the working capabilities of a handy boatman. Moreover, as the boatman takes up any of these alterations he will acquire techniques—such as the fiberglassing of a shelf or the through-cutting of a hull —that will prove useful in doing any number of modifications of his own devising.

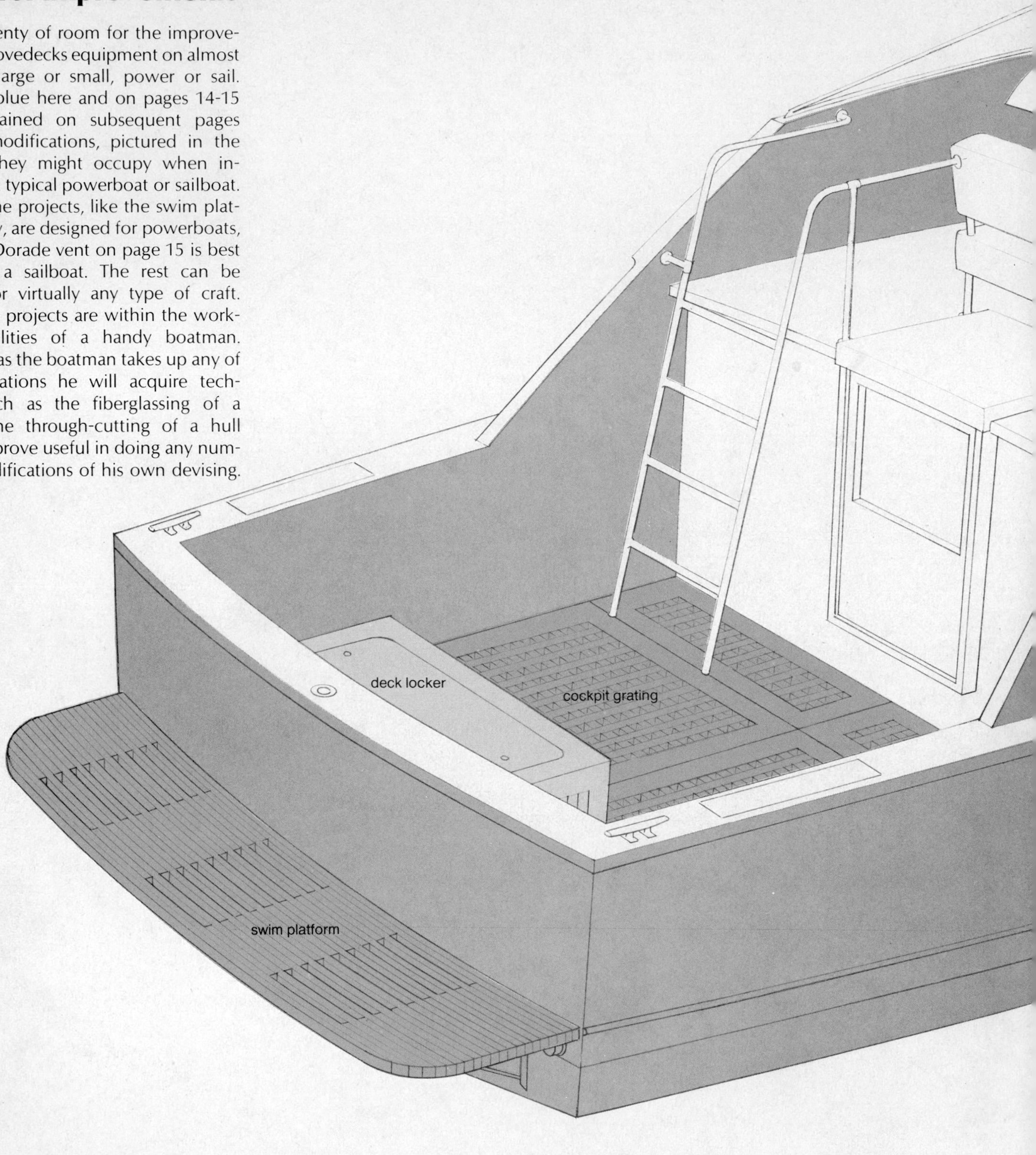

deck locker

cockpit grating

swim platform

Shown above are possible locations for six abovedecks improvements (blue) that a boatman might add to a 28-foot powerboat. They include a chrome handrail along the side of the cabin, a porthole that opens (pages 54-57), a platform attached to the transom for the convenience of swimmers (pages 38-43), and a depth finder whose transducer (pages 58-61) is attached to the underside of the hull.

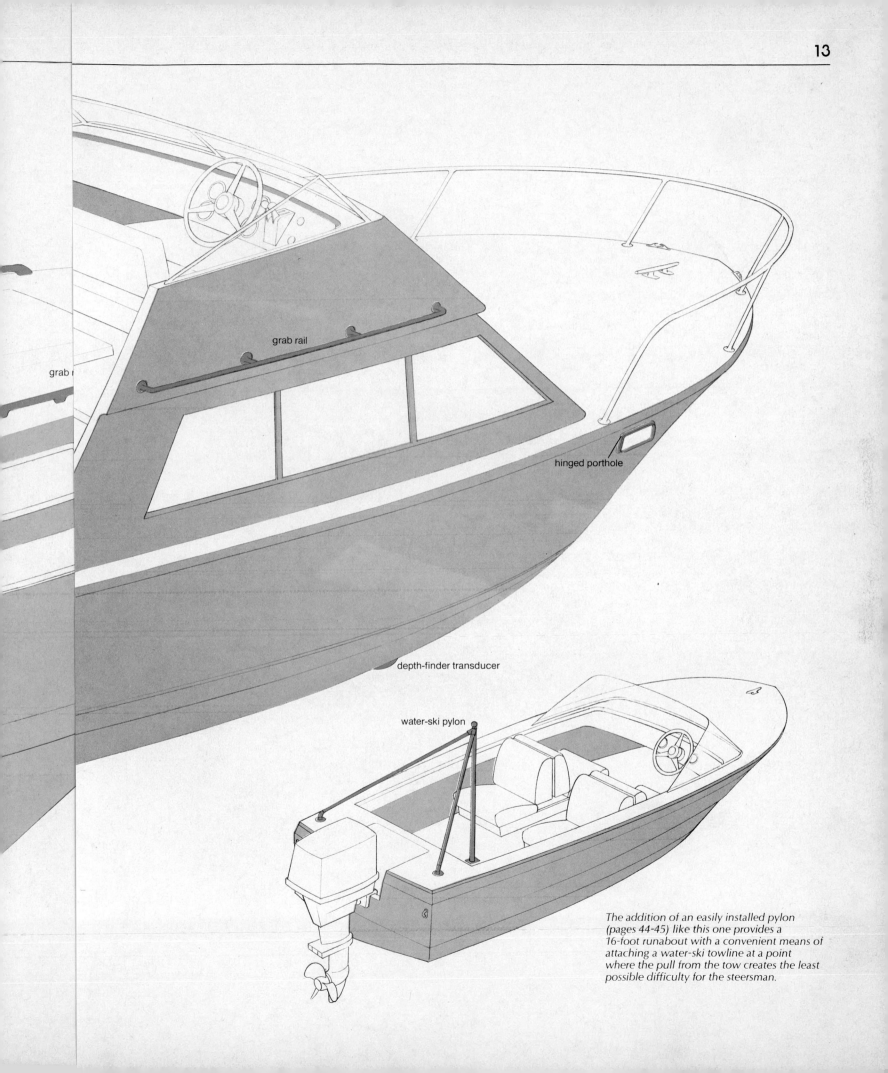

grab rail

grab r

hinged porthole

depth-finder transducer

water-ski pylon

The addition of an easily installed pylon
(pages 44-45) like this one provides a
16-foot runabout with a convenient means of
attaching a water-ski towline at a point
where the pull from the tow creates the least
possible difficulty for the steersman.

A Sturdy Grab Rail

Wood or metal grab rails are essential features on any cabin top, and a boatman can easily install them himself. Not only do these handholds provide a critical measure of safety in rough weather, but as any sailor knows, they also offer convenient surfaces on which to lash a swab or tie a wet bathing suit.

The rails for sailboats are traditionally made of wood—either mahogany or teak—and they can be purchased ready-made and in various lengths up to 12 feet. Rails for powerboats are either stainless steel or chrome-plated bronze or brass; the required posts and tubing are available separately to make a rail of any length. The wood varieties usually require that the boatman drill holes into them for bolts, using a jig *(below, right)* as a guide; metal rails come with the holes cast in them.

The procedures detailed here and on pages 18-19 describe the process for putting a wood rail on a fiberglass boat. As when making any through-deck installation in fiberglass, a key step is the placement of a reinforcing doubler between the liner and the deck. This doubler anchors the deck bolts and prevents the liner and deck from cracking under strain. Such installations should also be finished below with some sort of decorative cover—like the teak panel described on page 19. If the rails are to be installed on a canvas- or fiberglass-over-plywood cabin top, neither reinforcement nor panels are needed; rail bolts go directly through the sturdy deck and are cinched tight against the cabin top (only full-thread bolts should be used on any boat). In any case, make sure there are no fittings or wiring in the path of the saw.

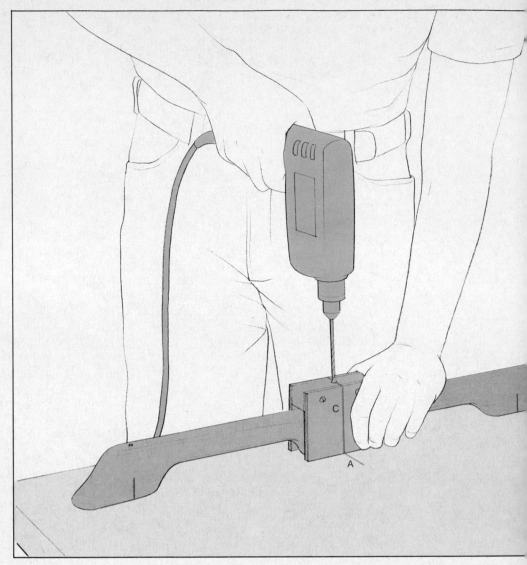

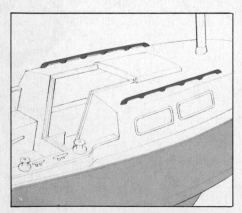

Grab rails are mounted lengthwise and opposite each other on a cabin top. To install them, begin by positioning each rail so that it lies at least three inches in from the cabin's edge. Then, with a helper holding one end of the rail, mark the rail's position by tracing the rail footings at either end. Mark on the rail the center point of each footing.

A Jig to Steady a Drill

The best way to hold a drill bit perfectly vertical when drilling through a curved narrow surface like the top of a rail is through the use of a jig *(right)*.

To make such a jig, cut a rectangular block from 1¼-inch hardwood, making it four inches long and the exact width of the rail. Cut two sides for the jig from ¼-inch plywood, making them four inches long to match the block, and as high as the rail plus the block's thickness. On the top of the block draw two lines connecting opposite corners; the point at which the lines cross is the center (B). Secure the block in a vise. At the center, drill a perpendicular hole using a drill press with a bit to match the diameter of the bolts you will use later in securing the rail. Clamp the block and its sides together, and drill two smaller holes through all three pieces. Bolt the sides to the block. To complete the jig, draw a guideline (C) from the block's center to one long edge and from there straight down the side.

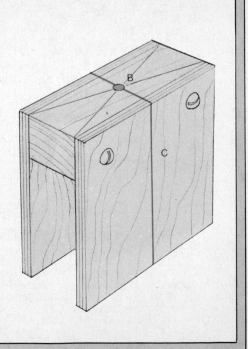

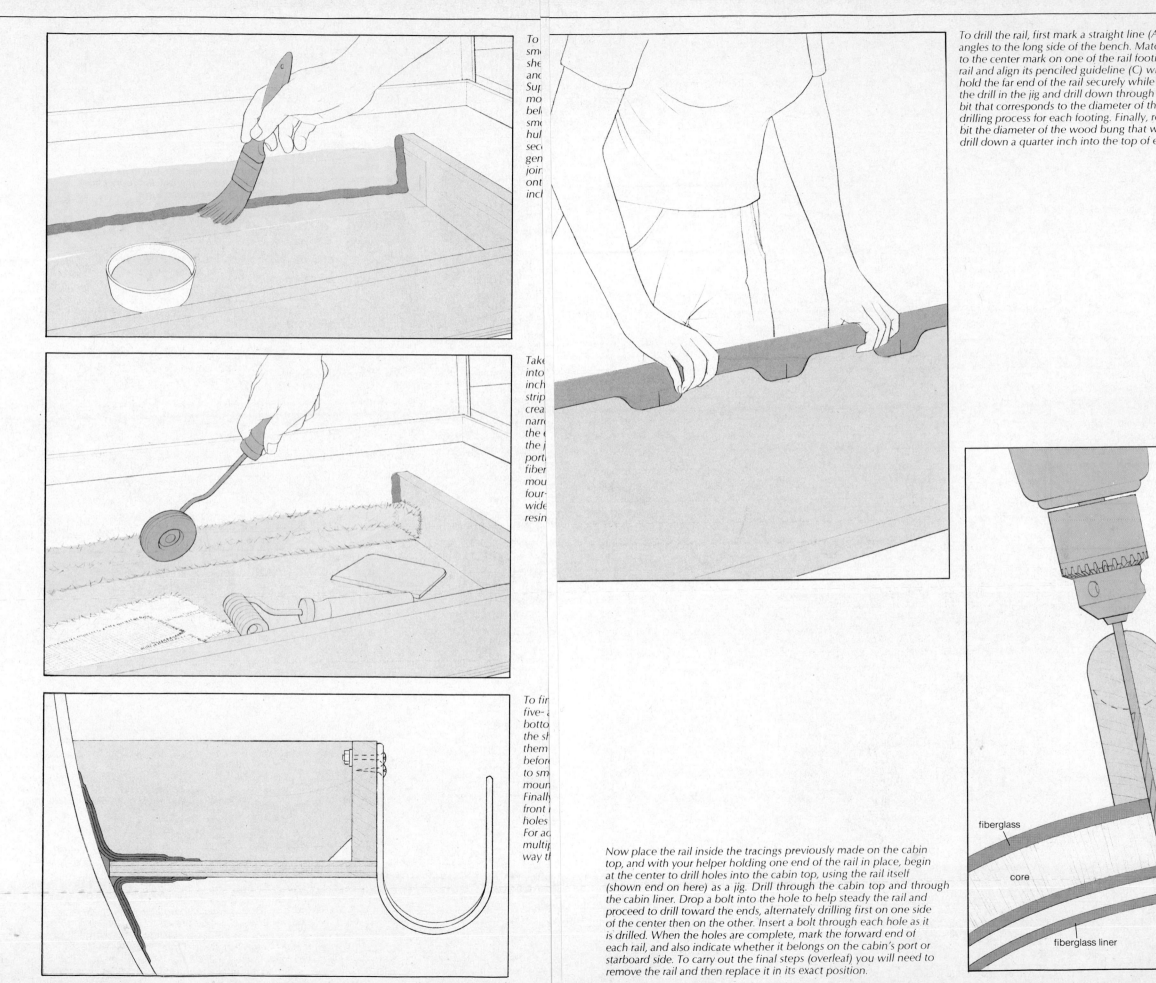

To drill the rail, first mark a straight line (A) on a workbench at right angles to the long side of the bench. Match the line on the table to the center mark on one of the rail footings. Slip the jig over the rail and align its penciled guideline (C) with line A. Have a helper hold the far end of the rail securely while you hold the jig. Then set the drill in the jig and drill down through the rail to the table, using a bit that corresponds to the diameter of the bolt shank. Repeat the drilling process for each footing. Finally, remove the jig, change to a bit the diameter of the wood bung that will cover the bolt head, and drill down a quarter inch into the top of each hole.

grab rail

fiberglass

fiberglass

core

fiberglass liner

Now place the rail inside the tracings previously made on the cabin top, and with your helper holding one end of the rail in place, begin at the center to drill holes into the cabin top, using the rail itself (shown end on here) as a jig. Drill through the cabin top and through the cabin liner. Drop a bolt into the hole to help steady the rail and proceed to drill toward the ends, alternately drilling first on one side of the center then on the other. Insert a bolt through each hole as it is drilled. When the holes are complete, mark the forward end of each rail, and also indicate whether it belongs on the cabin's port or starboard side. To carry out the final steps (overleaf) you will need to remove the rail and then replace it in its exact position.

A Convenient Shelf

The utility of storage space aboard a boat can be enormously improved by putting in a shelf for holding the small, hard-to-find objects that otherwise clutter the dank recesses of cockpit lockers. Such shelves are doubly useful if equipped with hooks or brackets, to accommodate such items as lines and snatch blocks. The most useful hooks are the blunt type with rounded ends normally used on deck to hang life rings.

Making and mounting such a shelf is easy, even on a fiberglass boat, which requires bonding with fiberglass strips and resin rather than the simple screws used on a wooden vessel. A practical shelf size would be 32 inches long and 9 inches wide with a 4-inch-high rail. But requirements vary, and the boatman will want to adjust both dimensions and structural details to fit the available space.

The most workable shelving materials are ½-inch marine plywood for the bottom and one-inch white or sugar pine for the rail. The wooden parts should be joined together with 1½-inch flathead brass or stainless-steel screws. Usually the assembled shelf will be mounted on the curved surface of some part of the hull. This means that its back and sides must be drawn and cut in subtle curves that abut perfectly on the mounting surface. The keys to proper curves are a carpenter's compass and a set of cardboard templates (right), basic devices that can be used to install not only shelves but cabinets, lockers, or any other object the boatman wants to attach to his boat's hull.

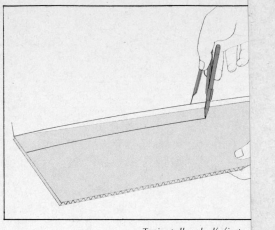

*To install a shelf, first sa_____
length guideline on the h_____
a vertical line at each e_____
shelf on the guidelines. N_____
vertical as shown, trac_____
the cardboard along the _____
of the she_____*

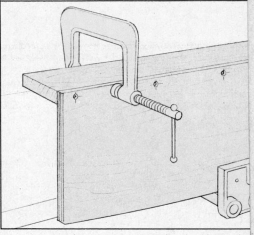

*Clamp the front rail a_____
screw holes centered_____
spaced at about five-_____
them, and glue the she_____
Then scr_____*

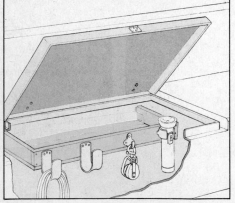

A particularly handy place for a shelf like the one described on these pages is inside a cockpit locker, where a boatman needs to store dozens of vital tools and parts that must come quickly to hand when he needs them.

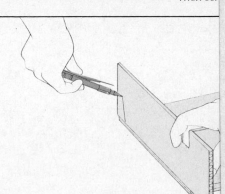

*To create side rails wit_____
cardboard strip as high a_____
shelf and scribe the c_____
parallel with the shelf. R_____
it back in place. Draw a l_____
of the front rail. Remov_____
Use the template to cut t_____
bottom front corner_____
Then mark, drill and scre_____*

A Cockpit Grating

One of the most useful and showy improvements a boatman can undertake is a cockpit grate like the handsome teak model shown here. It helps to keep feet dry when water splashes aboard and adds a custom-built touch to any vessel.

The grate consists of a rectangular grid of interlocking notched or dadoed wood strips surrounded by a solid wood frame to which it is fastened by dowels. Runners are attached under the length of the grate —two runners down each side if, as is commonly the case, the cockpit has watershed troughs; if not, a third runner goes down the middle. The wood for the project is cut from ⅞-inch teak planks, which should be ordered four inches longer than the length of the cockpit.

Three specialized pieces of equipment are essential to milling the teak—a drill stand, a circular table saw and a radial arm saw, preferably with a ¾-inch-wide carbide-tipped dado head or multiple carbide-tipped saw blades with spacers. While these tools exist in only a few home workshops, they may be rented or found at a nearby high school's shop. If not, many lumberyards will do the required milling to order.

The key to constructing a grate is the measurements, which must be entirely worked out ahead of time on a diagram like the one at right. This allows the boatman to establish the outer and, much more importantly, the inner dimensions of the frame, so he can calculate and cut the correct number of ¾-inch-wide strips needed to create the rectangular grid. An additional preliminary step, required for an irregularly shaped cockpit, is the making of a paper template, which is then set aside until the finishing stages, when it is used to trace the cockpit's shape onto the frame; the frame is then sawed to fit.

A teak grate can be made to fit well into almost any cockpit. The grid is always rectangular, but the solid teak frame can be shaped precisely to fit the cockpit structure.

24"

37"

grid

frame

To prepare a working diagram, first measure the cockpit's length and width and subtract ⅛ inch all around for clearance. In this case the outer dimensions are 37 inches by 24 inches. The frame sides must be at least two inches wide at the frame's narrowest point, allowing for taper (dotted line). They may be as much as six inches wide, depending on preference. Figure out a grid of ¾-inch strips and ¾-inch spaces, shown here as blue shading. Arrange the grid so that a space always adjoins the frame (if the alternating strips do not come out exactly, adjust the inner dimensions of the frame accordingly). In this example, the frame's interior dimensions turn out to be 30¼ inches and 17¼ inches, and the grid is made up of 20 short strips and 11 long ones.

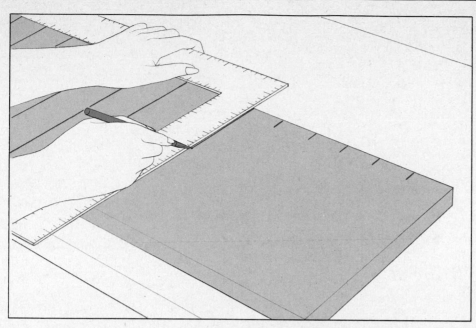

Cut the frame pieces to the measurements on the working diagram. Ignore tapering at this stage, but make sure to square the ends. Now cut two runners equal to the length of the grate and the depth of the cockpit's watershed troughs; if your boat does not have troughs, cut three ¼-inch-high runners. In doing so, set the table saw at an angle so the runners are ⅞ inch wide at the top and ½ inch wide at the bottom. Now along one side of each remaining board, mark precise 1½-inch intervals. With an L square and a retractable utility knife, score lines across the boards exactly at those intervals.

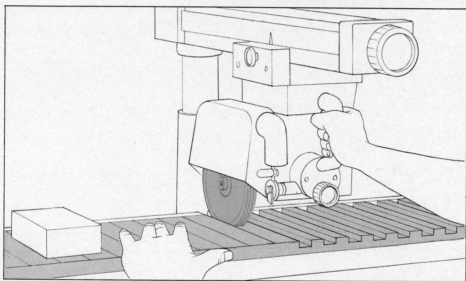

Adjust the vertical position of a radial arm saw, equipped with a ¾-inch-wide dado head or multiple saw blades, to cut exactly halfway (⁷⁄₁₆ inch) through the thickness of the teak board and make sure the blade is perfectly upright. Test the cut on a scrap of hardwood and adjust the saw if necessary. Align the left side of the saw blade with the first scored line on one of the marked boards. Place a heavy weight such as a lead brick near the cutting area, as shown, to prevent the board from bowing up as it is cut. When finished you should have alternating rows of ¾-inch-wide dado blocks and notches.

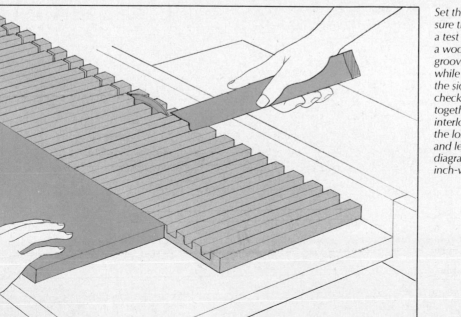

Set the table saw for a ¾-inch cut, making sure that the blade is perfectly vertical. Make a test cut on a scrap of hardwood. Now, using a wood prod as shown, feed each of the grooved boards lengthwise into the saw, while a helper guides the teak board from the side with a plank. Occasionally, double-check the cuts by fitting several strips together crosswise. The grooves should interlock snugly without forcing. Finally, cut the long strips into the number of crosswise and lengthwise pieces determined on the diagram. Make sure that all end with a full ¾-inch-wide dado block.

When all the strips have been cut, place each of the crosswise strips, notched side down, on a drill stand. Using a counterbore bit for a No. 6 screw, drill through the center of each notch. Then lay all the grid strips out, one alongside the next with the notches up, and brush them with teak oil, which will act as a lubricant when fitting the pieces together.

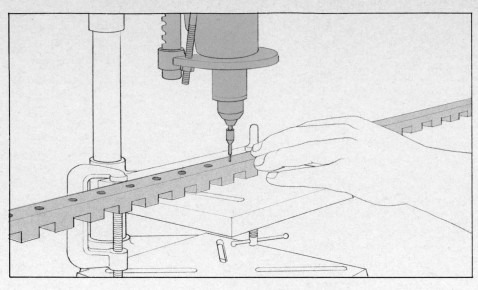

To interlock the grid strips, lay parallel all the lengthwise strips notched side up. Insert a single crosswise strip, notches down, across one end. Tap it in place with a wooden mallet or set a board on edge over the strip and pound it with the mallet. Add one or two more crosswise strips next to the first, then a crosswise strip at the opposite end. With the grid now fairly stable, add the other crosswise strips. If a strip seems to stick going in, find where it is binding and sand it down. If any of the dado blocks breaks off, save the piece, and glue it back in place with resorcinol after all the strips have been interlaced.

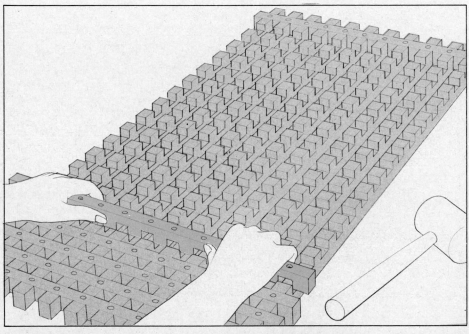

Drop a No. 6 ½-inch flathead brass screw into each of the holes. Tap the screws gently with a mallet to set them. Finish screwing by hand or with an electric screw driver.

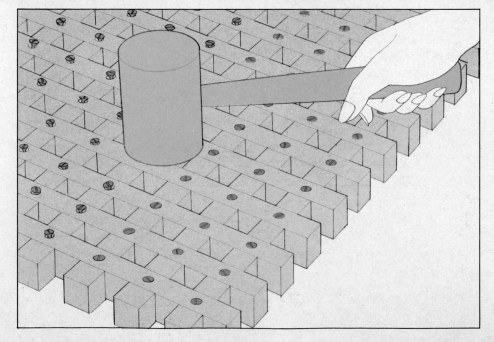

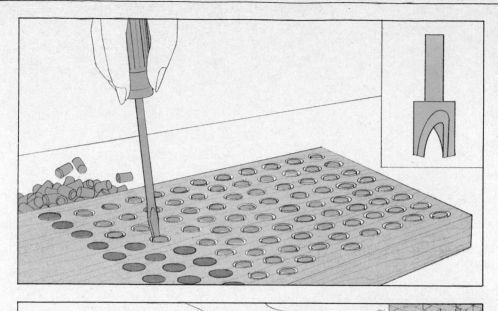

Make bungs for the screw holes, drilling them out of teak scraps with a plug bit (insert) the size of the screwheads. Flip the bungs out of the board with a screw driver as shown, being sure to push against the grain of the wood. (If you do not wish to make your own teak bungs, you can purchase them from a marine-supply store.) Plug the holes by dipping an end of each bung in resorcinol, aligning the grain of the bung with the grain of the strip and tapping it into place.

Sand the grid's surface with a belt sander, using No. 100 sandpaper. Work back and forth the length of the grid until the teak is smooth and the bung tops are flush with the surface.

To attach the frame, begin by centering one of the short frame pieces along a short end of the grid. Using a carpenter's square, draw a line through the center of the end of each grid strip and its corresponding point on the frame. For ease in assembly later, write matching pairs of identifications (A, A) indicating match-ups between grid and frame side. Mark the other edges of the grid and the other frame pieces the same way, using a different letter to identify each side. Where the frame pieces connect, make a mark on each piece or move dowels, as necessary.

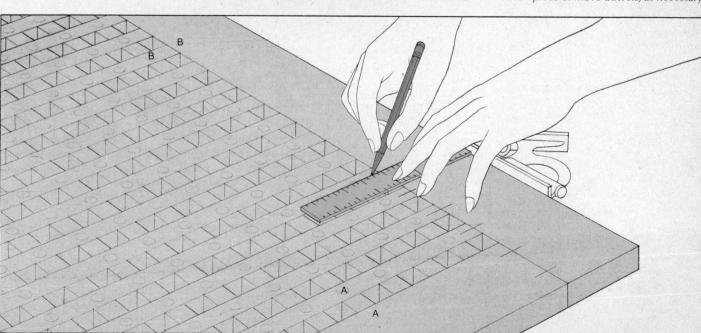

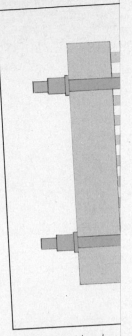

Clamp the grid and en...
together with pipe clar...
frame pieces. Use thre...
them alternately above...
pressure and prevent t...

If tapered frame...
cut, trim ⅛ inch...
template to allow...
template in plac...
cuts with a sabe...

To assemble the grid and
grid with the pencil-mark
edge of the workbench a
bench with two C clamps
jig on the near end of on
using the pencil mark dra
step as a guide. Clamp d
a ⁵⁄₁₆-inch hole to a depth
Repeat on all the remain
moving the jig as you pr

Clamp one of the fram
with the pencil-marke
to the edge of the ber
doweling jig to the fra
hole to a depth of ½ i
marking. Next insert a
each hole after dippir
into resorcinol. Tap th
wood mallet until the
for the remaining fra

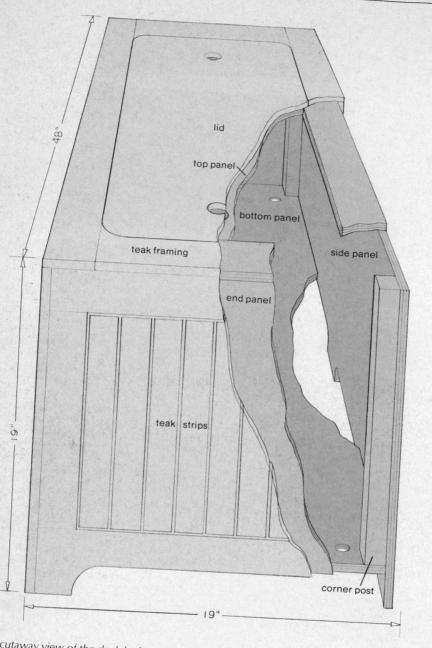

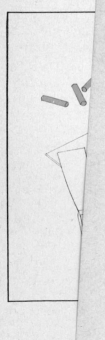

A cutaway view of the deck locker reveals its sandwich construction
—a ½-inch marine-grade plywood interior and a facing of ½-inch-thick
Burma teak strips. The plywood components can all be cut from a
single 4-by-8-foot sheet. They are: two panels measuring 47 by 18
inches for the sidepieces; two 17-by-18-inch panels for the end
pieces; a 46-by-17-inch panel for the bottom; and another 47-by-18-
inch panel for the top. (For ease of handling, the boatman may want
to order these panels precut at the lumberyard.) The four teak corner
posts are each 15 inches long; they do not extend down into the legs.
Instructions for cutting the teak facing—both the ½-inch-thick framing
pieces for the top and the vertical strips—are on pages 36-37.

A Dual-Purpose Locker

On powerboats that have large, sheltered cockpits, a freestanding deck locker provides convenient storage for bulky, frequently used gear. With the addition of a cushion, it becomes a comfortable bench. The locker shown here measures 48 inches long by 19 inches wide by 19 inches high; its structure, as diagramed at left, is of two layers: a plywood interior and an exterior facing of teak. A pair of 1¼-inch holes in the top allow the boatman to poke a finger inside to remove the lid, and smaller holes located in the bottom at each corner allow any water that may seep inside to escape.

Construction begins with the plywood interior, which has six major components: two long side panels, two shorter end panels, a panel for the top and one for the bottom. Before assembling these pieces, the boatman must make cutouts along the side and end panels to create six curved legs. He then fits all six panels together, bracing the corners with 1-by-1¼-by-15-inch support posts, as shown, and coating all surfaces with resorcinol glue before screwing them together. When the top panel is screwed in place the boatman cuts out from it the locker's large access opening; the cutout piece is then overlaid with an outer layer of teak whose edges protrude beyond those of the cutout to form the box's lid.

After the basic box and lid are completed, the boatman cuts the teak facing. Planks for the top are simply fitted on and glued around the lid. He then makes certain that strips for the side are set on evenly spaced and vertical, with sealant applied to the surfaces between them to simulate deck caulking.

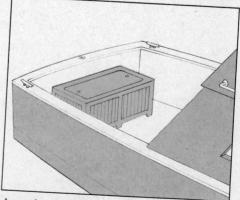

A good spot for the cockpit locker is against the rear bulkhead of the cabin, as here, or against the transom—where it is handy to a crewman but more exposed to the weather. In either place, the locker can be bolted to the bulkhead, or else affixed to the deck.

First mark one plywood side panel with guidelines for cutting out legs. Inscribe a horizontal line two inches above the bottom edge—the height of the legs. Next draw a vertical line—the width of a corner leg—two inches in from the panel's side. To make the curve of the leg, set a compass at 1½ inches and inscribe an arc that fairs into both lines.

On the same panel, mark guidelines for the leg at the other corner, using the same measurements as for the first leg. Next, draw guidelines for the middle leg. Begin by determining the mid-point of the board (23½ inches from either end); then draw vertical lines one inch to either side of the mid-point and inscribe arcs similar to the ones at left on either side of the verticals.

Following the guidelines, cut out the legs with a saber saw and sand their edges. You can now use this panel as a template for inscribing guidelines on the second side panel. When you have done this, make guidelines for corner legs on both of the end panels, using the same set of procedures.

To begin assembling the locker's major plywood components, first clamp one of the corner support posts in a vise with the one-inch edge facing up. Glue a plywood end piece to it with resorcinol, aligning the top side of the post with the panel's top and edge. The post will not reach the bottom of the panel, but will end three inches above the point where the leg begins. Drill three screw holes through the panel and into the post —one at each end of the post and one in the middle. Set in and tighten the screws. Affix a second corner post to the other edge of the panel. Repeat with the second end panel.

After both end panels have been fitted with corner posts, put on the locker's side panels, as shown, gluing all joints and holding the assembly together with pipe clamps. Drill screw holes through the side panels and into the post, staggering them so as not to hit the screws already set into the post to fasten down the end panels.

Set a screw into each corner leg to hold it together. Drill the screw hole near the bottom of the side panel where it overlaps the end panel, ¼ inch in from the edge. The screw will then bisect the ½-inch thickness of the end panel.

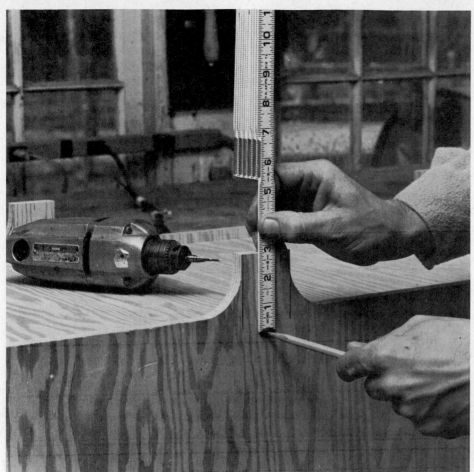

Turn the locker upside down and drop in the bottom panel so that it rests securely on the ends of the corner support posts. Glue and screw the panel onto the four supports. Next, on one of the side panels, measure down 2¼ inches from the end of each leg and connect the measurements with a horizontal line. The line represents the middle layer of the bottom plywood panel, along which screws must be inserted for reinforcement. Drill at spaced intervals along this line, through the side panel and into the bottom. Repeat for the other three panels. Set and then tighten the screws.

Lift the plywood lid clear, sand it lightly along the edges and set it aside. Now drill and fasten the fourth edge of the top panel to the side panel underneath, checking first that the process of screwing down the top's other three edges has not caused the side panel to bow inward. If necessary, have a helper reach inside the box and press outward to bring the side into alignment.

Turn the locker right side up; place its top panel in position. Drill screw holes centered on each corner post; glue and fasten down the top, setting screws along three of the top's four edges. Prepare to cut out the lid. Inscribe a guideline 3½ inches from each end and three inches from each side. Insert a saber saw along the line as shown; proceed to cut out the top (right).

Now apply the locker's teak facing, starting with the side panels. From a ½-inch-thick teak board, cut a piece 18½ inches long and four inches wide as trim for the bottom of the panel. Turn the locker on its side and put the piece along the bottom. Trace the panel's curving leg design on the underside of the teak. Cut out the shape. Reposition the teak, glue, and clamp in place, protecting the teak from the clamps with wood buffers. Counterbore three screw holes; set in the screws. Cut and apply lengths of teak to trim the other three edges of the panel. Repeat on the other side panel and two end panels.

Cut 44 teak facing strips, all 1¼ inches wide and 11¾ inches long. Begin laying them on one of the sides within the trim. Block each strip along the top, bottom and sides with ¼-inch plywood spacers, as shown. Work from either end of the locker toward the middle. Leave a 3⅜-inch-wide space in the middle of each side panel; this is to make room for a piece of 2⅞-inch planking that will act as a center divider. Finally, cut out the center divider, glue and screw the strips and divider into place. Remove the spacers. Repeat the process on the remaining sides, but omitting the divider on the end panels.

Cover all exposed teak surfaces on the locker's sides and ends with masking tape. With a caulking gun, squirt black polysulphide-base sealant into the troughs between the teak strips. After filling each trough, smooth the compound until it is flush with the taped surface, using a putty knife. Leave the tape in place until the compound hardens—about five days.

Cut out enough teak planks to completely cover the locker's plywood lid, leaving a ½-inch overlap in all four directions; the overlap will provide a lip to keep the lid from dropping through its hole into the locker top. Sand the edges between each teak plank, where necessary, to ensure a snug fit. Glue the teak to the plywood lid and counterbore screw holes around the perimeter of each piece; screw down the teak. Round the corners of the teak with a saber saw, using a compass curve like the one on the plywood part of the lid.

Set the finished lid into place and cut two 2-by-48½-inch lengths of teak to fill or frame the space between the long sides of the lid and the edges of the top panel. Fasten these down. Then remove the lid, invert it and trace the shapes of its two ends on two 14½-inch-long teak planks. Cut out the traced shapes with a saber saw and sand to mate the shapes of these new cuts perfectly with the short edges of the lid. Put these shaped pieces in position as end frames, and fasten down. Set teak bungs into every screw hole in the teak. Sand the locker with a belt sander.

To finish the locker, drill four ½-inch drain holes in the bottom, one in each corner; then, with a series of drill holes, cut two 1¼-inch finger holes in the lid. Round and smooth each hole cleanly with a file. Clean off all sawdust, and oil the locker with teak oil on a soft rag. To keep the finish in first-class shape, re-oil the locker every season.

A Perch for Swimmers

A practical and distinctive addition to almost any powerboat is a platform fixed to the transom to provide swimmers with a safe and easy way to get into and out of the water. The best of such platforms are made of inch-wide strips of teak, sawed from 1¼-inch-thick planks, and assembled together in such a way that they form alternate solid and open sections. The solid sections rest on supporting stainless-steel brackets. The open sections permit quick runoff of water and reduce strain on the supporting brackets by allowing waves to wash through rather than bang against the bottom of the platform.

A boatman building a swim platform must take a number of preliminary steps before he begins his carpentry. Since the platform has to conform to the curve of the transom, he must first construct a jig (opposite, top and center) that will reproduce exactly the transom's curvature. Next he computes the precise size and angle of the brackets that are required (opposite, bottom); these must be made up professionally in a metalworking shop. He then makes a paper template (page 40), defining the size and shape of the curved ends of the platform.

When setting about the actual construction, the boatman fastens a strip of teak onto the curved face of the jig. He then builds the platform outward by gluing and screwing together successive teak strips, carefully spacing the short strips that comprise the platform's solid sections. When the platform is finished, he bolts the lower legs of the brackets through the transom, and finally bolts the platform itself to the brackets.

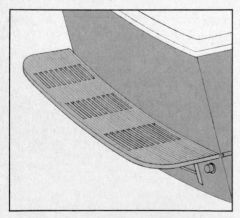

A typical swim platform like the one above is installed at the level of the boat's spray rail —if the boat has one—or 4 to 6 inches above the waterline. Brackets used to support the platform are positioned to avoid exhaust pipes.

This view shows the pattern of the teak strips in a swim platform, spaced to form both open and solid areas and bent to the exact curve of a boat's transom. This curve and that of the platform's rounded ends must be carefully designed. To calculate how much teak will be needed for the project, measure the width of the transom at the level at which the platform will sit. Add 6 to 8 inches, depending on how sharply the transom curves. Buy enough teak planks of this length to cover the width of the swim platform itself, plus 4 inches to allow for breakage. Saw all strips full length; later cut the shorter strips.

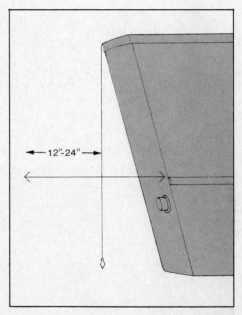

To compute the width needed for a platform on a raked transom, drop a plumb line from the top of the center of the transom. Measure the distance from transom to plumb line at the level at which the platform will be installed. The width of the completed platform should be the sum of this distance —plus the amount of usable platform width desired. The usable widths of most swim platforms range between 12 and 24 inches.

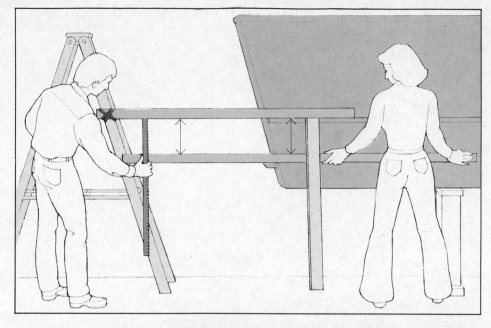

Making a wooden jig of the transom's curve against which the platform is built begins with the erecting of a scaffold. Prop one end of a 5-foot, 1-by-2 board against the hull at the level at which the platform will rest. While a helper holds a length of batten precisely at the waterline, adjust the board by a series of careful measurements between it and the batten (left) until the board and the batten are parallel. Nail or tape the free end of the board to a support such as a ladder. Repeat the process on the other side of the transom.

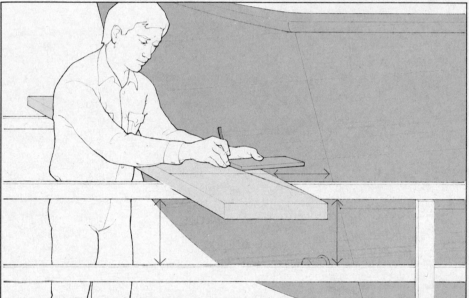

Lay a plank of 2-by-12 construction lumber a foot longer than the width of the transom across the 1-by-2 supports, with the mid-point of the plank touching the transom's center and its ends equidistant from the transom's outside edges. Make sure the supports are still parallel with the waterline. With an L square mark the ends of the transom across the plank. Hold a square block of wood about 8 inches long against the transom and hold a pencil vertically upright against the block's other end. Now move the block along the full width of the transom, carefully scribing the curve of the transom onto the plank.

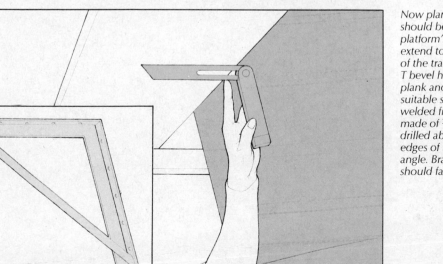

Now plan the brackets. Their upper legs should be 2 inches shorter than the finished platform's width; the lower legs should extend to within 2 or 3 inches of the bottom of the transom. Find their angle with a T bevel held between the underside of the plank and the transom's center (left). A suitable stainless-steel bracket (inset) can be welded from 1⅛-inch angle stock with a brace made of ¾-inch pipe. Order ⅜-inch holes drilled about 3 inches apart along the inside edges of the legs starting 2 inches from the angle. Brackets for the ends of the platform should face inward to hide the bolts.

With a saber saw, cut along the curve marked on the plank to make the jig (above) for the platform. Divide it with lines perpendicular to its straight edge into sections corresponding to the solid and open portions of the finished platform. Label each section "solid" or "open." (Widths of the sections may vary, but the solid sections at the ends must be at least 12 inches wide to accommodate the curves, and those in the center at least eight inches wide for strength.)

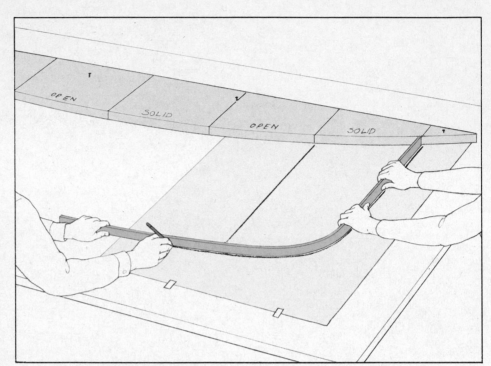

To make a template for the platform's rounded ends, lay one end of the jig on a large sheet of paper that is taped to a workbench. With a ruler, extend onto the paper the line that marks the inside edge of the solid section at one end. Make the extension as long as the width of the finished platform. Have someone hold one end of a batten against the line on the jig marking the end of the platform. Bend the batten to touch the end of the line on the paper. Adjust to your liking the curve of the batten. Trace on the paper the curve of the batten (right). Cut the paper along this curve.

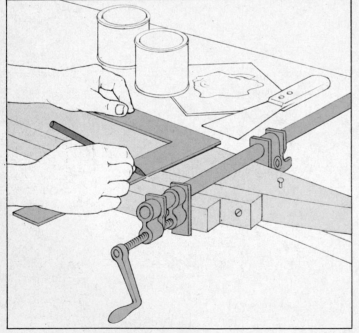

Nail or clamp the jig atop a workbench. Clamp first one end, then the middle, then the other end of a long teak strip to the jig. Let the ends lap three inches over the end marks for the platform. Screw the strip to the jig 1½ inches from each end with No. 10 screws 2½ inches long. Remove the clamps, spread resorcinol along the exposed side of the strip, clamp a second strip to the first and anchor it with screws one inch in from the ends. Where each solid section will be, drill three evenly spaced 1½-inch-deep holes; insert 1½-inch stainless steel screws, marking their locations on the strip's upper surface. Extend across both strips the lines dividing the sections (above).

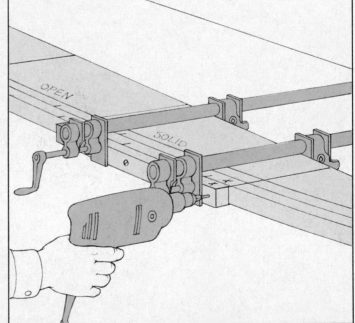

Now cut and clamp in place a strip of teak about an inch longer than one of the interior solid sections. Extend the guidelines in that section onto the strip. Mark the adjoining surfaces at one end with an "X." Unclamp the strip, cut off its ends as marked; apply glue to its inner side and reclamp it. Attach it with three 2½-inch stainless-steel screws, siting the screw holes (above) to avoid the screws that anchor the adjoining strip. Attach short strips where other solid sections are to be built up, letting the outside ends of strips in the two end sections extend two inches beyond the platform's end lines. Mark all screw locations. Keep the surfaces of the strips level as they are joined.

Complete a row of short strips along the full length of the platform. Apply glue to their outer edges. Then attach another long strip. Continue alternating rows of long and short strips, making sure the ends of the short strips align; as an aid, extend the section guidelines onto each long strip as it is added. As you attach strips at each end, use the paper template to mark out the platform's rounded ends so no screws are placed outside that curve. End with two long strips.

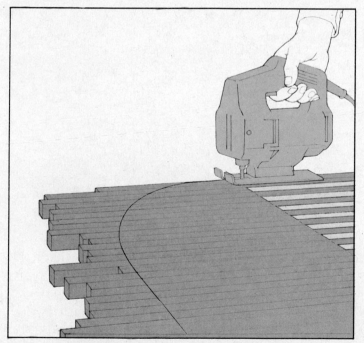

Detach the jig from the bench. Rough-sand the top and bottom surfaces of the platform across the grain with a belt sander. Then rough-sand the top and bottom with the grain. Next, fine-sand the top and bottom with the grain. Now, carefully trace the curve of the paper template onto each end of the platform. Cut around the curves with a saber saw (above). Be sure to support both the jig and the platform during this part of the operation, since the cuts through the innermost long strips pass inside the screws holding the jig to the platform and will therefore release the platform from the jig.

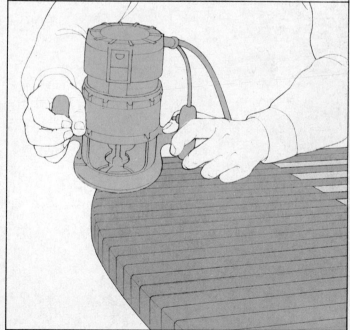

To make a quick, neat job of smoothing and rounding the outside top and bottom edges of the platform, use a router with a 3/8-inch-radius, corner-round carbide bit. Run it along first the top and then the bottom edge, holding the router flat against the surface of the platform (above). Then fine-sand the rounded edges by hand. Alternatively, all of this finishing can be done by sanding.

Start installing brackets by placing the top of
one end bracket on a line marking the level
of the platform's bottom. Hold the bracket
vertical, within the curve of the platform and
clear of any exhaust pipes. Mark and drill ⅜-
inch holes through both the transom and a ½-
inch-by-4-inch-wide plywood doubler. Apply
bedding compound to the lower leg of the
bracket and the inner face of the doubler.
Attach the bracket and doubler, using
stainless-steel bolts with hex heads for ease
in tightening. Put washers between the
boltheads and the bracket, and washers and
lock washers between the doubler and nuts.

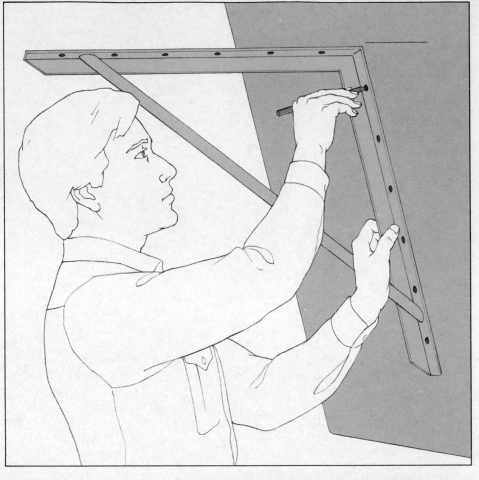

After installing the two outside brackets,
center the platform across them ¼ inch away
from the transom and check to make sure it
lies level fore and aft. This can be done by
having a helper hold a long batten parallel to
the waterline while you measure the vertical
distance from the batten to the front and
back of the platform. If the platform is not
parallel to the waterline, shim it into
alignment by placing thin strips of teak
between the platform and the brackets, as
shown below. Now attach a bracket under
each solid section, using the same techniques
as in mounting the two end brackets.

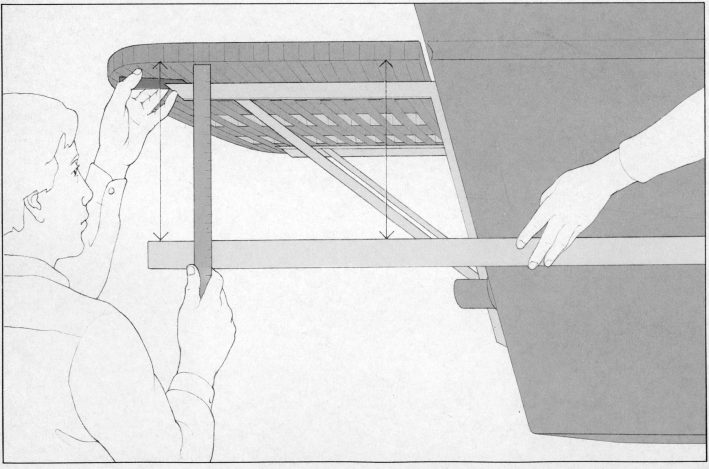

As a cushioning measure, drill the holes for the bolts that attach the platform to the brackets with a bit slightly larger than No. 6 bolts. Drill up through the holes in the end brackets first, as at left. Drop No. 6 round-head bolts in these end-bracket holes to hold the platform steady. Then drill similar holes for the other brackets.

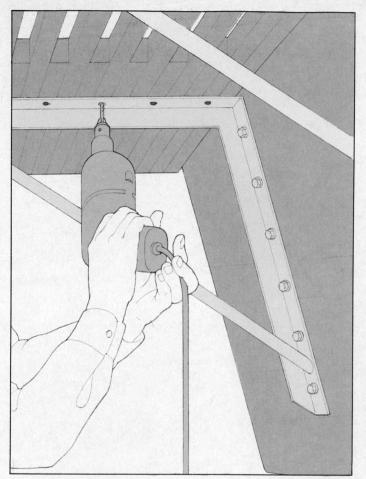

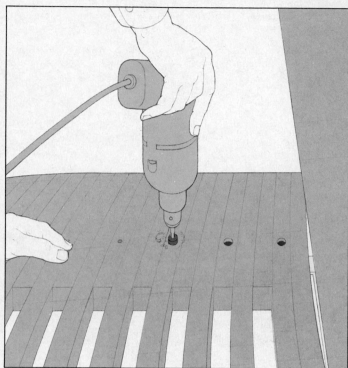

To finish the platform, plug the bolt holes with teak bungs. Starting with the inner brackets, drill down through each hole with a counterbore bit the size of the boltheads. Drop in the bolts and tighten them using washers and lock washers. Repeat for the end brackets. Tap glue-dipped bungs into the holes, aligning the grain of the bungs with the grain of the platform. Sand off the projecting tops of the bungs. As a final touch, the platform edge can be protected by screwing on a 1-inch half-round molding of stainless steel, aluminum or bronze.

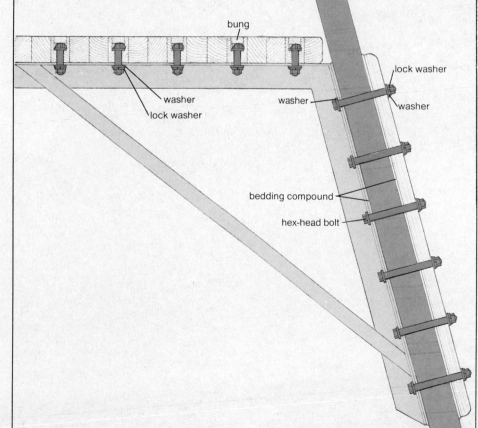

bung

lock washer

washer

washer

washer

lock washer

bedding compound

hex-head bolt

This cross section of the installed swim platform shows the final positioning of both the round-head bolts and washers holding the platform to the brackets and the hex-head bolts and their washers holding the bracket and its doubler to the transom.

A Rig for Skiing

The best tow rig for water-skiers is an aluminum pylon *(below and at right)* that can be snapped in and out of on-board mounting brackets. The pylon has two prime advantages over the more common, stern-mounted yoke rig *(below, right)*. Because the pylon is mounted close to the boat's center of gravity, sudden, lurching pulls from the weight of a zigzagging skier are less likely to influence the ski boat's course and stability. Secondly, when the skier's towline is attached to the top of a pylon, the line has free vertical and horizontal movement. This reduces the occurrence of sudden sags and tension in the line, both of which can throw a skier off balance and impair a boat handler's control over the craft.

Though there are minor variations in the designs of pylons, the great majority of them are of the basic tripod configuration shown here, and can be quickly installed, as demonstrated. And on days when the towboat is not being used for skiing, but rather as an ordinary runabout for picnicking or fishing, the pylon can be demounted by removing the pins at the ends of its arms and slipping the base of the pylon out of its mounting plate.

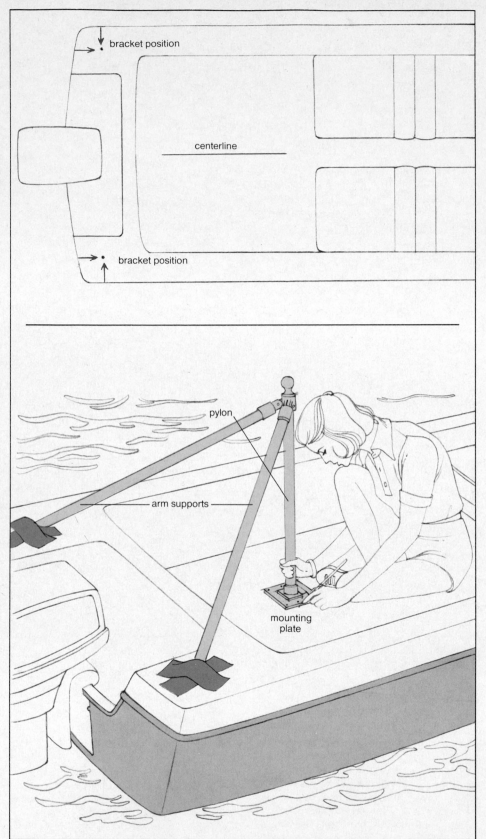

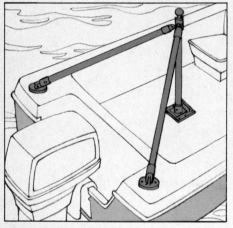

A ski-tow pylon like this one should be mounted on the centerline of a boat near enough to the stern that its arm supports reach flush deck space near each quarter. The 1¼-inch aluminum piping and all fittings that fasten the assembly together and to the boat may be obtained as a ready-made package from a variety of marine-supply outlets.

To mount a towing pylon on a fiberglass ski boat, find two clear and reasonably level spots in the same relative position on either quarter of the boat and mark the spots with tape. Then locate and mark the craft's centerline. Next, position the arm supports on the predetermined mounting topots, temporarily holding them in position with more tape. Stand the pylon, attached to its mounting plate, on the boat's centerline perpendicular to the floor boards; check to see if the arm supports spread at least 45° and mark the position of the pylon support plate (below).

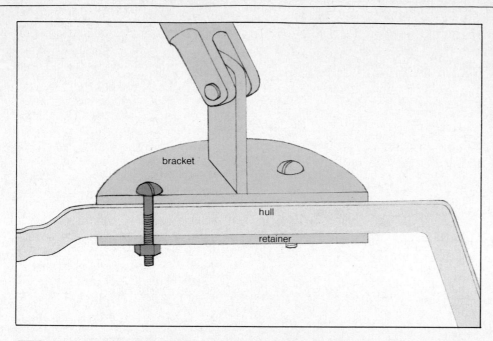

With the pylon and arm supports in place, start securing the assembly, beginning with the quarter brackets that hold the ends of the pylon's arm supports in place; these are bolted through the fiberglass hull and backed with metal retainers. To install, put each bracket in turn on the spot determined at left, and drill bolt holes through the deck. Drop the bolts through the bracket and the hull; reach under the deck and place the retainer beneath the bracket so the bolts fall through the plate's holes. Fasten each nut with a wrench on the bolthead above the deck and one on the nut beneath.

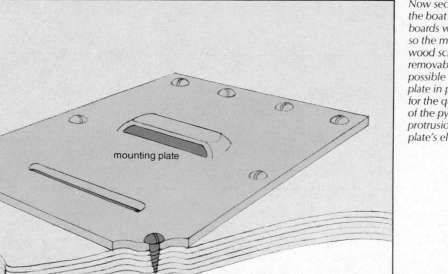

Now secure the pylon's mounting plate to the boat's floor. In most boats the floor boards will be of permanently fixed plywood, so the mounting plate must be fastened with wood screws. If the boat's floor boards are removable, however, or if it is otherwise possible to reach beneath them, bolt the plate in place by the method shown above for the quarter brackets. Now secure the butt of the pylon to the plate by slipping the flat protrusion at the base of the pylon under the plate's elevated cowling.

A Quick and Easy Bridle

A simple stand-in for the ski-tow pylon is the water-skiing bridle, consisting of a length of polyethylene line, holding a free-running block, and attached at either end to eyebolts protruding from the hull. Most modern runabouts come equipped with transom eyebolts; they serve as trailer tie-down attachments and as dock-line dead ends, as well as tow eyes. However, if a boat is not equipped with eyebolts, they are obtainable from almost any marine-supply store. Find two spots equidistant from the upper corners of the transom, as far apart from each other as possible. Drill the spots and drop the bolts through the holes; back them with doublers and wrench the bolts tight. The method for making the bridle itself is demonstrated on page 128.

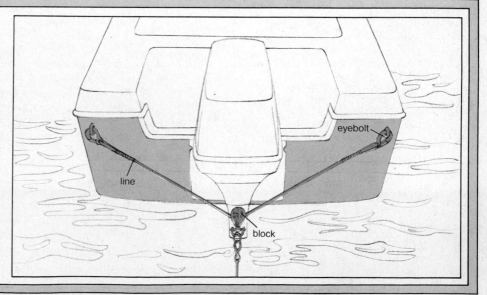

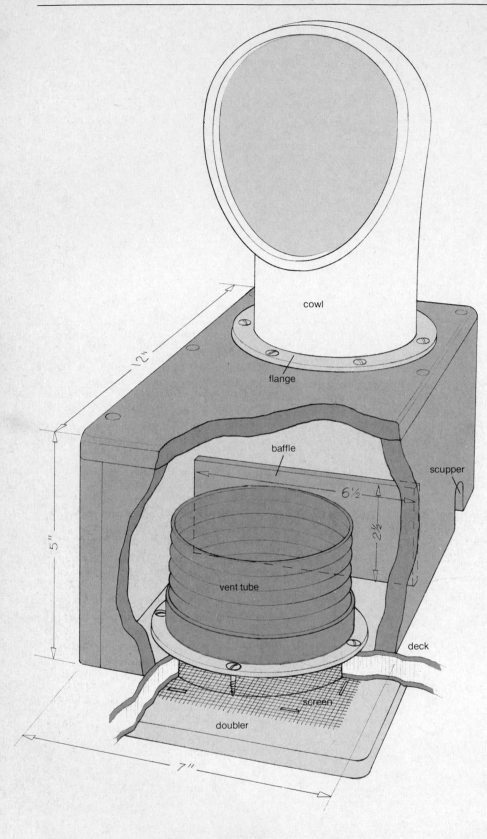

cowl

flange

baffle

scupper

12"

5"

6½

2½

vent tube

deck

screen

doubler

7"

A Fresh-Air Vent

To ventilate a stuffy cabin without letting in water—even in high seas and stormy weather—skippers use Dorade vents like the one at left. Named after the 1930 ocean racer on which it was developed by designer Olin Stephens, the Dorade vent's key feature is a box mounting with an interior baffling system that blocks rain and sea water from getting below.

An industrious boatman can build and install a Dorade vent on his boat in two weekends. The dimensions of the box, constructed from ½-inch teak and joined by screws and glue, must be large enough to accommodate a flexible plastic ventilator cowl. These cowls, with two-to-six-inch base sizes, are available at marine-supply stores. The interior baffle should be made of ¼-inch marine plywood and glued to the box by a strong and leakproof dado joint—a rectangular groove cut in one piece of wood so that another piece can butt into it at right angles.

To guarantee an adequate flow of air, a hole equal in diameter to the vent cowl must be drilled through the deck of the boat. A special hole-cutting bit—for attachment onto a heavy-duty electrical drill, can be purchased inexpensively for this step—and greatly simplifies the task. Alternately the job can be done by drilling a circle of six or eight small holes with a standard drill bit and cutting out the inside disk with a saber saw.

Since Dorade boxes are installed in exposed positions abovedecks, every joint and fitting must be carefully sealed with waterproof glue to prevent leakage.

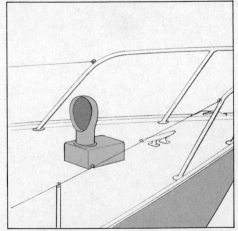

This cutaway view of an installed Dorade vent with a 4-inch ventilator cowl shows how the interior baffle deflects rain and sea spray, yet provides a steady supply of fresh air. The face of the cowl can be rotated in its plastic flange to face the direction of the wind. Air entering the 5-by-7-by-12-inch box passes around the baffle and circulates belowdecks through a rubber vent tube. Water splashing into the cowl cannot reach the lip of the vent tube, and drains out a side scupper. A wire screen, set between the vent tube and a doubler belowdecks, prevents insects from entering the cabin.

A Dorade ventilator on the foredeck of a cruising sailboat provides air for the forecastle, a notoriously stuffy place aboard ship. This vent has been installed just aft of the anchor cleat, to ensure that its hole does not cut through the major supporting member to which such fittings are secured.

In constructing the Dorade box, first cut the top and sides to the proper dimensions. Then make a dado joint in the sides to receive the baffle. To create this joint, measure and mark the mid-points of the two longer sidepieces with a ruler. Then take a combination square, like the one at left, and draw two parallel lines on each board to indicate where the dado groove will be; one line should be at the mid-point of each sidepiece and the other exactly ¼ inch away.

Cut the groove for the dado joint either with a radial-arm saw set to dig ¼ inch into the teak sidepiece, or with a backsaw. In using a radial-arm saw, position the sidepiece so the saw cuts just inside one of the marked edges. Then saw back and forth, moving the sidepiece over slightly after each cut. In using a backsaw, make a ¼-inch-deep cut on each line, then chisel out the intervening wood.

With the dadoes finished, coat the ends of the plywood baffle with waterproof glue and wedge them into the grooves on the sidepieces. Then secure the assembly with a clamp and let dry.

With the baffle tightly in place, begin assembling the rest of the Dorade box. Coat the end pieces with glue and clamp them securely, one at a time, inside the side pieces of the box. Then, using a counterbore drill, make screw holes at evenly spaced intervals through the side pieces into the end pieces. Be sure to use bronze or stainless-steel screws that will resist corrosion.

Cut bungs from wood dowel rods to fill the counterbored holes above the screw heads. Dip the bungs in waterproof glue. Use a wooden sculptor's mallet or a block of hard wood to pound the bungs into the holes.

Smooth down the tips of the wooden bungs with a belt sander like the one at right. On a comparatively small job like this, if the boatman does not own a belt sander, a hand file and sandpaper will suffice—though they take more time.

Now prepare to saw a hole for the vent cowl in the completed Dorade box. First, with a compass inscribe a circle—in this case four inches in diameter—on the top piece of the box. Then drill a ¼-inch hole at any point along the circumference of the circle, and cut out the hole with a saber saw, as at left. Finally, saw scupper holes in the bottom edge of the box below the vent cowl.

After sawing out the scupper holes, varnish the box completely, both inside and out, to protect it from weathering. Apply two or three coats, allowing 12 hours for each coat to dry before installing the box on the boat.

When the box outline has been marked, draw the inside dimensions of the box with a right-angle ruler. Then mark positions for 10 through-deck mounting holes. Precisely position the opening for the large vent hole through the deck. The mid-point of the hole should be one half the distance from the inside of the box's forward end to its inner baffle—and centered along its length.

To install the assembled Dorade vent on the foredeck, first position it in a spot that will allow it to circulate fresh air throughout the cabin below. But the abovedecks position of the box must not interfere unduly with the movement of crew members when the boat is underway or at anchor. When the spot has been determined, mark the outline of the box with a pencil.

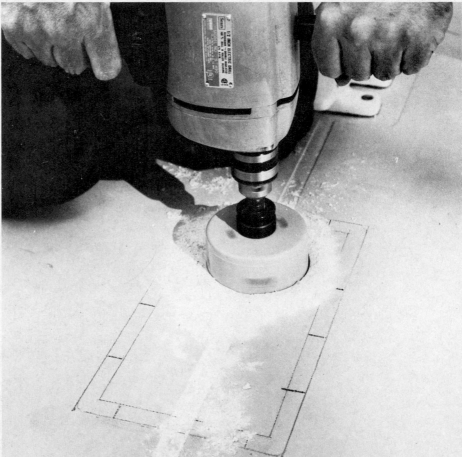

Cut the four-inch vent hole through the foredeck with an electric drill. The best tool to create a hole this size through a typical 1½-inch teak-reinforced fiberglass deck is the heavy-duty drill shown here with a special cutting bit attached. Without this special bit, the job can be done—more laboriously—by making six or eight small holes around the circumference of the vent hole and cutting out the inside piece with a saber saw.

Drill the 10 mounting holes through the deck at the positions marked on the outline of the box. A small block of wood, with a hole drilled ⅛ inch from its side, makes a handy jig for exactly centering each mounting hole. Line up the edge of the block with the outline of the box. Then guide a drill bit through the block and into the deck.

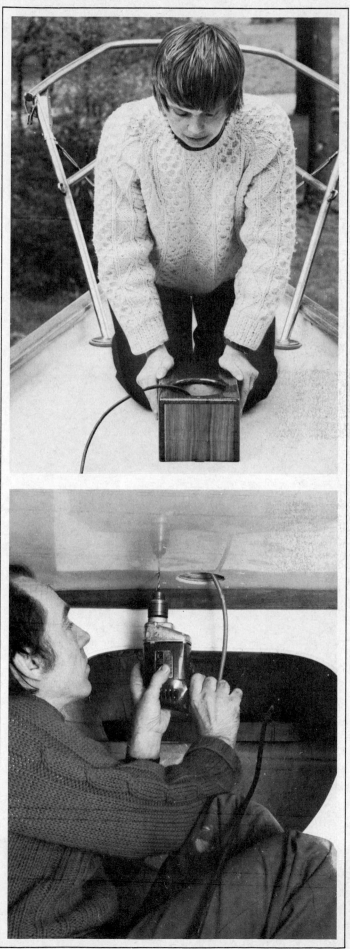

Now drill screw holes in the Dorade box to prepare for its final installation. To make sure the holes in the box match up with the mounting holes on the deck, go into the cabin; guide the drill back up through the mounting holes into the sides of the box (lower picture) while a helper (upper picture) holds it in place on deck.

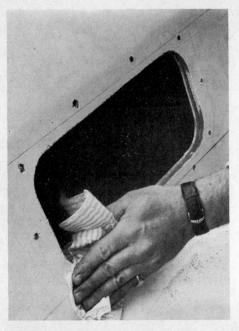

To prepare for final installation, remove the porthole assembly, and wipe down the bulkhead area inside and outside the opening with an acetone solvent to remove any fiberglass shavings. Also clean the metal assembly, using solvent if the light is glass, or soap and water if it is clear plastic.

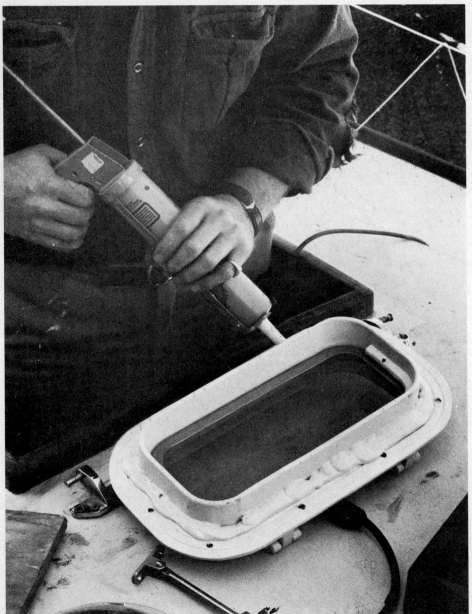

With the aid of a caulking gun apply a heavy layer of rubber-based, nonhardening waterproof sealant to the inside porthole unit, running the sealant along the junction between the flange and the frame.

Have a helper belowdecks replace the inside porthole unit in the opening and hold it firmly against the cabin bulkhead. Apply sealant outside along the crack where the projecting flange and the exterior cabin bulkhead meet. Reposition the outside rim and press it tight against the cabin.

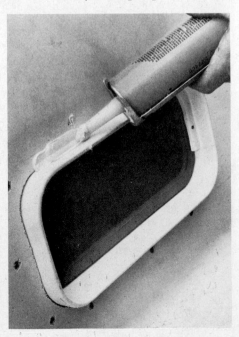

Have your belowdecks helper reinsert three long bolts in their holes while you tighten the nuts outside. This will hold the assembly steady during the task of affixing the cap nuts to the permanent bolts. Now have the helper insert the permanent bolts in the remaining holes while you tighten the permanent cap nuts. Remove the long working bolts and finish the permanent bolt installation.

Gently clean off the excess sealant around the port assembly with a putty knife, taking care not to scratch the finish. Wait two days for the sealant to set and wipe away remaining smudges of sealant and pencil marks with the solvent. If your window is plastic, be sure not to touch it with the solvent, which may permanently mar it.

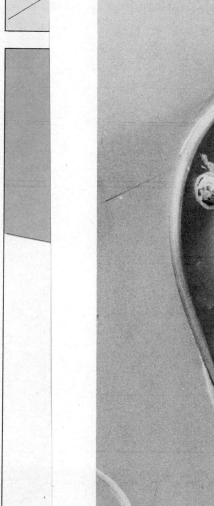

A G

A peri
the or
transd
—elec
with c
and ar
tem is
The t
receiv
that a
time l
echoe
on a d

A b
es the
the h
when
it mus
tions f
boatm
stem.
housir
hull, u
hold t

Afte
the fit
corder
the en
ence f
corder
the he
corder
sole.
cockp
way o
overle
the re
the el

*In the
sailboa
throug
directi
toward
arcs sh
bottom
and tra
mount*

2 There are few boats that cannot use an additional light for the cabin or chart table, or whose safety could not be improved by hooking up a bilge-water or gas alarm. With a few basic and inexpensive tools, such as a utility knife for stripping wire insulation, pliers, drill, screw driver and an electrician's crimper for joining wires together, any boatman can undertake such electrical projects himself, and achieve—in addition to personal satisfaction —considerable savings over the cost of professional installation. The basic electrical system on practically all boats is 12-volt direct current (DC) from the batteries. Some boats also carry a 110-volt alternating current (AC) sys-

ADDING ELECTRICAL EQUIPMENT

tem for hooking larger appliances into dockside power outlets; tinkering with this system is best left to a professional.

Installing a new DC fixture, however, requires little prior knowledge. The seaman needs to master the threading and attaching of various two-wire cables between the fixture itself and a service box or distribution panel, which disperses battery power throughout the boat. And he should have a basic understanding of the inner markings of the box. A typical box contains rows of terminals hooked to a set of fuses or circuit breakers that will automatically blow or flip off if too much current flows through them. The positive wire from the two-wire cable attaches to one of these fuses or circuit breakers. The negative wire hooks up to a terminal called a negative bus bar, which is normally placed within the panel, but on some systems is installed in a separate location nearby. A single wire leads from the bus bar to a grounding point on the engine block, where it connects with a negative wire from the battery to complete the circuit.

When hooking up wires, it is essential that the positive wire be fastened to the appliance's positive terminal and that the negative wire is led to the negative terminal—and similarly, to the positive and negative terminals on the box. Reversing the connections can seriously damage the device. To aid in identifying the positive and negative lines, the boatman should use color-coded wires. Manufacturers' color coding varies, but the authoritative American Boat and Yacht Council recommends that boat owners use red for positive, and black or white for negative. In addition, all boats carry a third wiring system, which bonds all major metal fittings such as water tanks and through-hull fittings to the engine block to prevent galvanic corrosion; the wires in this bonding system are normally green.

Choosing wire of adequate size is critical to the success of any electrical project. For the kinds of projects shown in this chapter, proper sizes are listed in the Appendix (page 168). The wire itself should be made of stranded copper designed to stand up to the constant vibration that might break solid wire, and its covering insulation should be moisture- and oil-resistant to withstand the damp environment on board.

New wire should be routed as high as practical above the bilge-water level, and secured about every 12 inches with a plastic or noncorroding metal clamp. When running several cables together, use plastic cable ties big enough to hold all the wires in a neat bundle. Whenever the cable passes through a bulkhead or some other obstruction, protect the insulation from chafing by installing a rubber bushing in the hole. Connectors that are used to fasten wires together and lugs that are used to screw wires to terminals should also be corrosion resistant.

One final word of caution: when installing any electrical device, wait until all other connections have been made before hooking the positive wire to the battery or service box; otherwise you risk a nasty shock.

A boatowner installing a VHF radio telephone screws an antenna's mounting plate onto a masthead. He will then lead a wire down the mast and through the cabin top to the radio.

Fitting in the Projects

Five electrical projects for a typical sail-boat and powerboat are outlined here. The new installations are in blue, as are the multiwire cables that carry power to them. The drawings have been simplified to eliminate electric installations already on the boat. But the existing wires between the service box, the battery and the motor are color-coded to indicate positive *(red)* and negative *(black)* wires. The green wire is the bonding wire that guards large metal objects, such as gas and water tanks, against electrolysis.

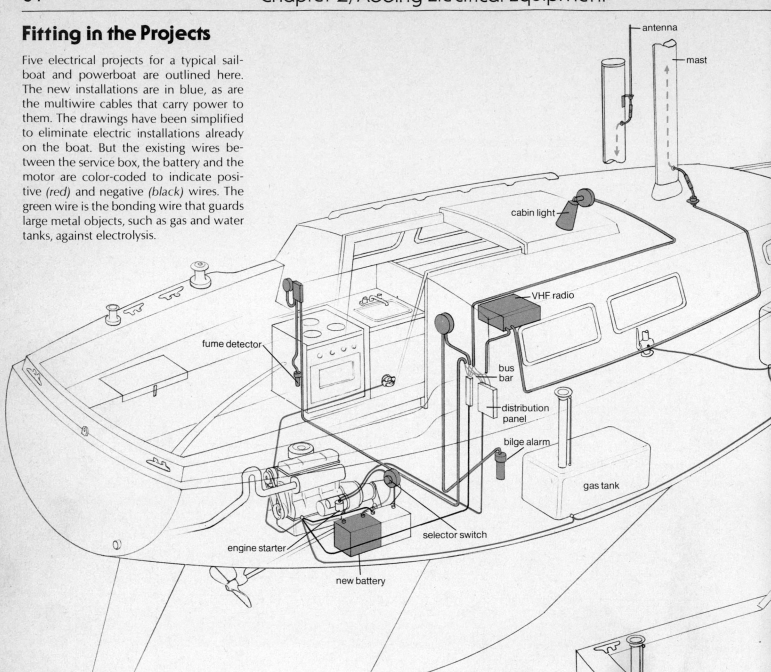

antenna

mast

cabin light

VHF radio

fume detector

bus bar

distribution panel

bilge alarm

gas tank

selector switch

engine starter

new battery

gas tank

Five projects for a sailboat, mounted in positions they might well occupy on such a craft, are: a VHF radio near the helm, with its wire running to an antenna screwed to the masthead; a fume detector beneath the stove; an extra cabin light over a bunk; a bilge-water alarm near the boat's center; a second battery and a switch for selecting between it and the original battery.

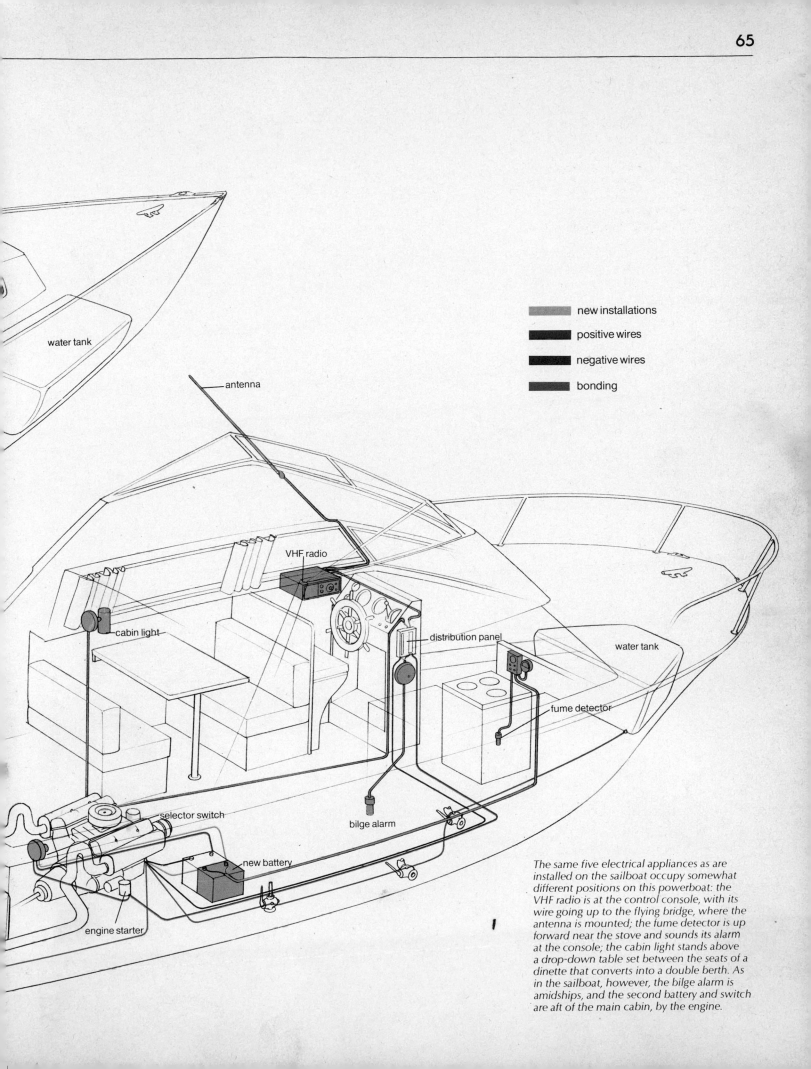

new installations

positive wires

negative wires

bonding

water tank

antenna

VHF radio

cabin light

distribution panel

water tank

fume detector

selector switch

bilge alarm

new battery

engine starter

The same five electrical appliances as are installed on the sailboat occupy somewhat different positions on this powerboat: the VHF radio is at the control console, with its wire going up to the flying bridge, where the antenna is mounted; the fume detector is up forward near the stove and sounds its alarm at the console; the cabin light stands above a drop-down table set between the seats of a dinette that converts into a double berth. As in the sailboat, however, the bilge alarm is amidships, and the second battery and switch are aft of the main cabin, by the engine.

Light Below

No electrical project is easier to install —or handier to have when finished—than an extra cabin light. Such a fixture is easily added to the bulkhead at one end of a bunk, or over a table.

The basic electrical system on boats operates on DC current, which does not lend itself to the installation of built-in outlet plugs. Therefore, new fixtures must be wired directly to the service box, or distribution panel, which is connected to the battery. This means threading the fixture's wire—actually a double wire that is normally color-coded red for positive and black for negative—around corners, behind bulkheads and under floor boards. This is easily done with a flexible wire tool called an electrician's snake.

The first rule in making such an installation—as in any other tinkering with electric wires—is to cut off the boat's electrical power by turning the battery selector switch (page 68) to "off." The second rule is to plan the project so that, in drilling holes and leading wires, obstructions such as plumbing pipes and reinforcing beams can be avoided.

If your distribution panel has two rows of terminals, one will be for attaching the negative wire and the other for the positive wire. If the box has only one row, as in the case of the installation shown on these pages, then all terminals on it are for positive wires; negative wires must be attached to a negative bus bar, which will be located nearby.

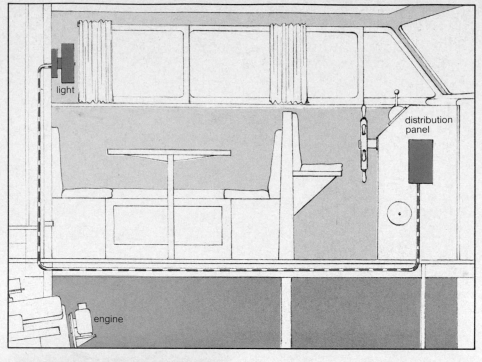

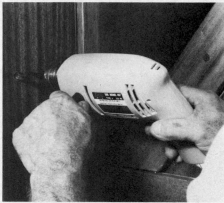

A schematic drawing shows the path of the cabin light's wiring. From the after side of the bulkhead where the light is mounted (upper left) the wire (dotted line) travels down between the bulkhead and a layer of paneling to the engine compartment, horizontally along the bilge and finally up to the distribution panel, located near the helm.

To mount a cabin light, begin by checking the other side of the bulkhead on which the light is to be placed to make sure there is nothing on the other side to impede drilling or snaking the wire. Then drill a hole in the bulkhead big enough for the light's wire to pass through.

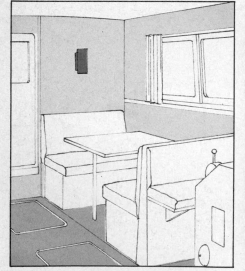

Mounted on a bulkhead over a bunk, this newly installed light illuminates one corner of the cabin for reading and idling belowdecks at night and on gray days.

Feed an electrician's snake through the hole you have just drilled, directing it down to the engine compartment. From there you will be able to manipulate the wire by hand.

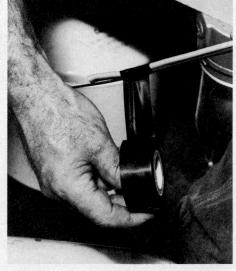

Go below to the engine compartment. Using electrical or masking tape, attach the end of the snake to the end of the wire, as shown; then cut off the excess tape.

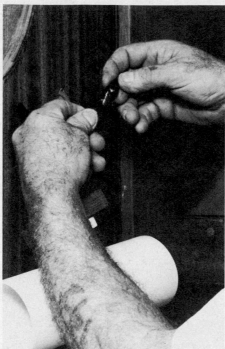

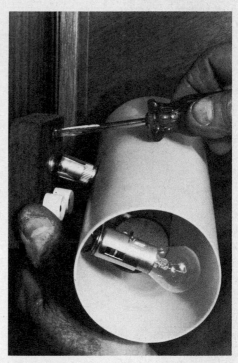

Return to the site of the cabin light and draw the snake back up through the drilled opening, bringing the electric cord with it. Then separate the snake from the cord.

Strip off some insulation from each of the cord's two wires. Using a butt splice connector, join the positive (red) wire to the lamp's positive wire and crimp the connection, using an electrician's crimping tool. Then join the negative (black) wire to the lamp's negative wire in the same way.

Carefully push the excess cord back into the hole and screw the mounting fixture for the light in its proper place on the bulkhead. Then return to the engine compartment.

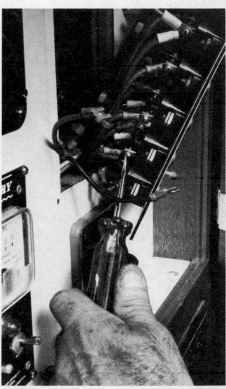

Along the main hatch beam in the engine compartment, secure the wire at intervals of about one foot with plastic clips so that the wire will neither flop nor tangle. Screw each clip into the beam. Then lead the wire up to the distribution panel, unscrew the panel and pull it away from the bulkhead, as at right.

At the distribution panel, strip the cord's insulation, exposing a half inch of negative and positive wires. Crimp a ring lug onto the end of each. Fit the positive wire's lug onto the back of the distribution box at the appropriate circuit breaker, and the negative one onto any open screw located on the negative bus bar.

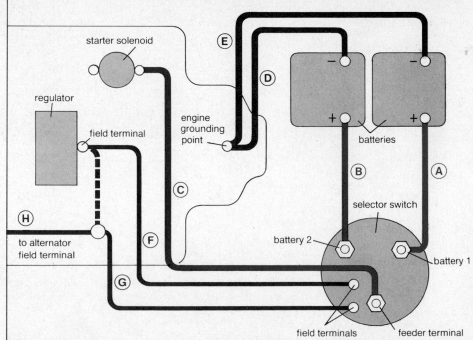

The best location for a second battery is alongside the first, close to the engine, to keep heavy cable lengths to a minimum. Make sure that each battery is in a ventilated, acidproof container, such as the plastic boxes shown above. These boxes come with a heavy strap to secure the box and its cover to the platform mounting underneath.

A dial in the face of the selector switch disconnects all battery power in the "off" position, and offers three "on" positions: battery No. 1 alone, both batteries together, or battery No. 2 alone. If the switch is turned to the "off" position while the engine is still running, the alternator is automatically disconnected, thus preventing a surge of voltage, which could burn out the alternator.

In this diagram for the switch, the power supply and return wires are represented by heavy lines. A and B run from the batteries to the switch; C joins the switch to the starter solenoid; D and E ground the negative battery terminals. The alternator cutoff circuit is shown in lighter lines. Wire H, from the alternator's field terminal, was previously (broken line) connected to the regulator; it is removed and joined to wire G from the switch. Wire F then replaces wire H on the regulator. The color-coded letters key the diagram wires to the actual wires in the following photographs.

Double Power

Most inboard-powered small craft come with a single battery that may be overloaded as new electrical gear is added to the boat. After a long spell of continuous use, as when the crew stays up late at anchor with the engine shut off, the battery may be too weak next morning to turn over the engine.

The simple addition of a second battery doubles the boat's power-storage capacity. And when a selector switch is added, as shown here and overleaf, the two batteries can be used—or charged—separately or together, depending on their condition and the vessel's current needs. For example, setting the switch's dial to "1" (left, below) while at anchor permits the No. 1 battery to be used to power lights and other accessories, while the No. 2 battery is reserved for engine starting. Should the No. 2 battery nevertheless become too weak to turn over the engine, a power boost can be provided by setting the dial on "Both," thus switching both batteries into the circuit.

When underway, the switch can be set in the same manner to direct recharging current from the alternator to either battery separately, or to both together. To prevent an alternator burnout, selector switches should also have an auxiliary switch that automatically shuts off the alternator when the batteries are cut off. The wiring changes for a cutoff can usually be made at the regulator, as indicated in the stylized diagram. If the regulator is inaccessible, consult the manufacturer's instructions for other wiring methods.

On the reverse side of the selector switch, locate the two large battery terminals—marked Battery No. 1 and Battery No. 2 on this model—and attach two positive battery cables (A and B) to these terminals. Tag each cable at both ends with identifying pieces of colored tape, which will serve as guides when you connect the cables to the batteries. Next, attach the starter cable (C) to the large terminal marked "Feeder" or "Common." Finally, attach two alternator cutoff wires (F and G) to the small terminals marked "Field" (either wire to either terminal) and tighten the terminal nuts.

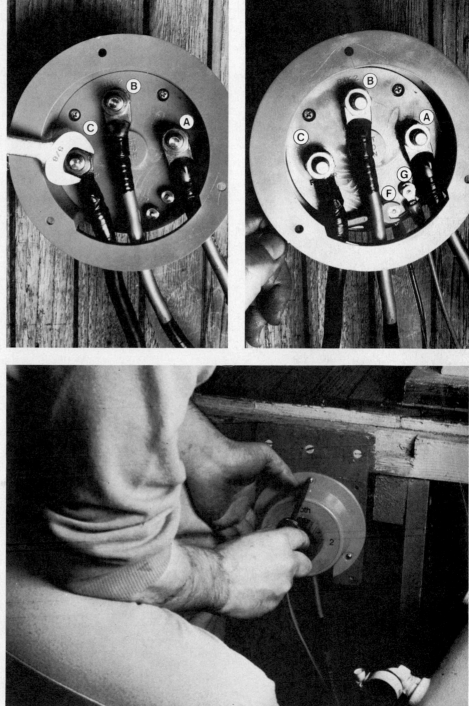

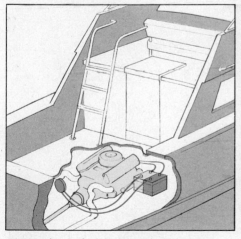

Mounted on a deck beam in the engine compartment, a selector switch, accessible through the engine compartment hatch, is placed close to both the old and new batteries to minimize connecting cable lengths, and to allow disconnection close to the power source in case of fire.

To mount the selector switch, first cut a rectangular backing plate from ¾-inch marine plywood. Using the switch as a template, place it on the backing plate and mark the position of each of its mounting holes. Drill pilot holes at those points and fasten the switch in place with the wood screws provided. Then drill three evenly spaced pilot holes across the top of the plate and secure the plate and switch to a deck beam with coutersunk wood screws. Tighten all screws an extra half turn to make sure that engine vibration will not loosen them.

To connect the heavy cable (C) from the selector switch to the engine, locate the starter solenoid and remove the nut and lock washer from its battery terminal. (Be sure not to disconnect the solenoid's other large terminal, which is located on the opposite side and is connected to the starter motor.) Then connect the starter cable (C) to the solenoid and tighten the lock washer and nut.

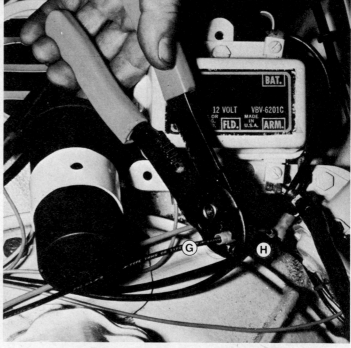

Hooking up the alternator cutoff circuit at the regulator is a two-step procedure, detailed in the photographs above and at right. First locate the regulator's field terminal (F or FLD. marking) and remove the existing wire from the alternator (H) by loosening the screw terminal. Then fasten one of the two wires from the switch's field terminals (F) to the vacant regulator terminal.

Clip off the terminal lug from the disconnected wire (H) and strip half an inch of insulation from the wire end. Similarly strip the second wire (G) from the switch's field terminals. Place the bared ends of both wires in a crimp-type splice connector and secure the connector at each end. Wrap the connection with electrician's tape.

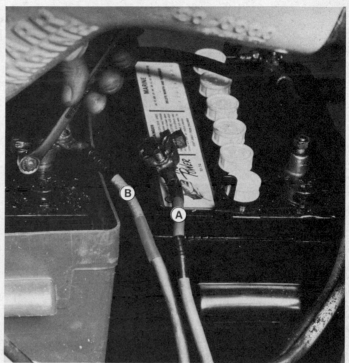

Before connecting the negative battery cables (D and E), make sure that the negative terminal posts on the batteries and the negative cable lugs are clean and corrosion-free. Secure the cables to the terminal posts by tightening the nut on each cable lug with a box wrench. Then connect the ring lug on the other end of each cable to the large bolt on the transmission housing that serves as the engine's grounding point. Tighten the grounding point bolt.

The final wiring step is to connect the positive battery cables (A and B) to the battery terminal posts. Double-check that the selector switch is in the "off" position and that the terminal posts and cable lugs are clean; then, using the colored tape applied earlier (page 69) as a guide, attach the cables from the switch's numbered terminals to the corresponding batteries. Tighten the cable lugs and then coat all four of the terminals with an electrically conductive paste or petroleum jelly.

For a neater and safer completed installation, use cable ties to harness the wires together under the selector switch, and wherever they run alongside other groups of wires near the regulator. Finally, check the operation of the new battery and selector switch by turning on a cabin light or other electrical accessory and making sure that the light stays on when the selector switch is in any of its three "on" positions, and that the light is off when the selector switch is turned to "off."

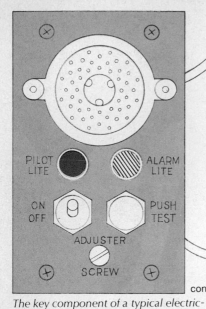

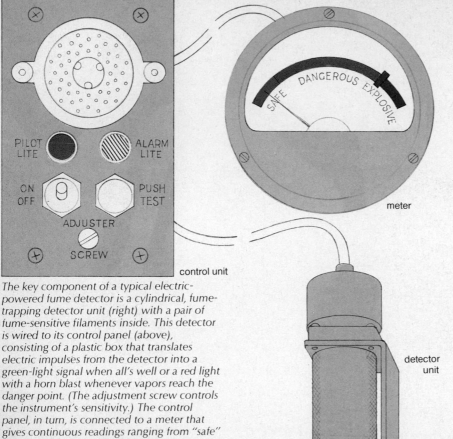

The key component of a typical electric-powered fume detector is a cylindrical, fume-trapping detector unit (right) with a pair of fume-sensitive filaments inside. This detector is wired to its control panel (above), consisting of a plastic box that translates electric impulses from the detector into a green-light signal when all's well or a red light with a horn blast whenever vapors reach the danger point. (The adjustment screw controls the instrument's sensitivity.) The control panel, in turn, is connected to a meter that gives continuous readings ranging from "safe" to "dangerous" or "explosive."

A Gas Sniffer

One of the wisest installations a boatman can make is a gas detector that will warn of toxic or potentially explosive fumes —either gasoline vapor from the engine, or cooking gas, as here—before they diffuse throughout the boat or settle in the bilge. A typical detection system like the one shown on these pages has three components: a detector unit, a control unit pretapped for mounting screws and a meter with mounting flange. All three components are wired to one another and to the boat's batteries.

The drawings here and overleaf show how to install such a detector next to a gas stove. Using these same basic steps, other detectors, hooked up to the control panel, can be placed near the fuel pump, carburetor or gas tanks—and an extra meter can also be wired onto a flying bridge. In addition, some boatmen take the precaution of installing a gas detector just above the storage batteries of the engine; these batteries tend to give off quantities of hydrogen gas when they are in the process of recharging.

After detectors have been installed, if the alarm sounds the boatman should instantly shut off his engine, close all gas valves, open doors, windows, ports and hatches, and turn off all electrical gear except for the bilge blowers—which are constructed in such a way that they do not generate sparks—until the leak can be located and repaired.

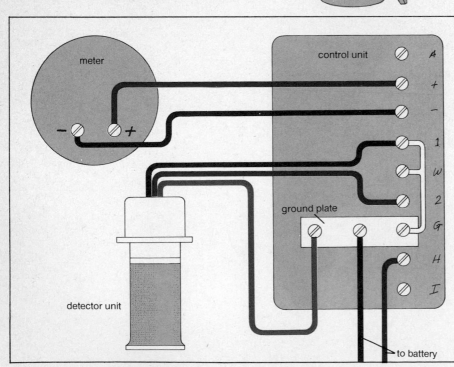

From the meter, a two-wire cable goes from the positive (red) and negative (black) terminals to the corresponding terminals on the control unit. A three-wire cable runs from the detector to the control unit: black wire to terminal 1, red to terminal 2, green to a terminal on the grounding plate (G). Power comes from the battery on a two-wire cable: black to the grounding plate, red to terminal H. When a single detector unit is used, terminals 1, W and G must be capped with another set of wires (white) fitted with resistors. The remaining terminals can be left vacant or be connected to extra units.

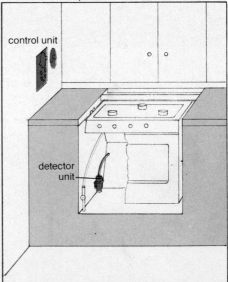

A fume detector mounted on the wall of the stove recess in a galley is placed low, where it is in the best position to give early warning of the presence of heavier-than-air cooking gases. Wires lead from the detector through the bulkhead to the rear side of the control unit, which may be located above and to the left of the stove, as here, or in some other place where it will be easily visible.

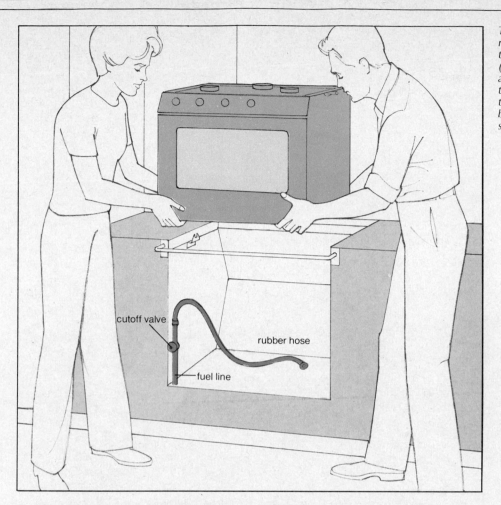

To install a fume-detection system, begin by removing the galley stove. First make sure that the gas is off, both at the storage tank (which by law must be carried in a ventilated area on deck) and at the cutoff valve where the fuel line joins the stove. Then disconnect the rubber hose from the intake nipple at the back of the stove and, with a helper, lift the stove off the gimbals.

cutoff valve

rubber hose

fuel line

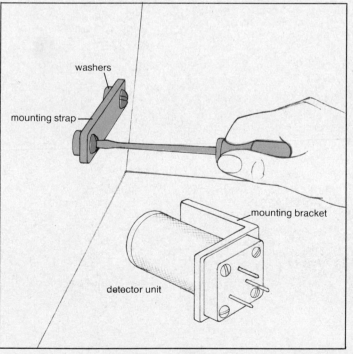

washers

mounting strap

mounting bracket

detector unit

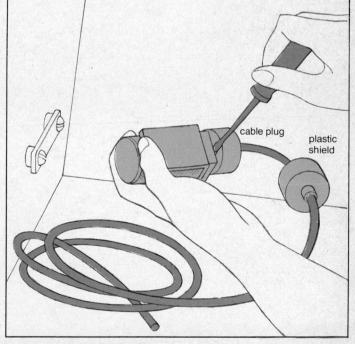

cable plug

plastic shield

Now attach the mounting hardware for the detector unit. To position the screw holes, use the mounting strap that comes with the unit as a template. On a side bulkhead of the stove recess, mark and drill pilot holes for two mounting screws. Then fasten the mounting strap and the two spacing washers to the wall with self-tapping screws.

Pull the plastic shield clear of the circular plug on the detector unit cable and loosen the three setscrews in the plug. Align the plug with the three pins located on top of the detector unit and push the plug into position. Tighten the setscrews to secure the cable to the detector and then push the shield back into position.

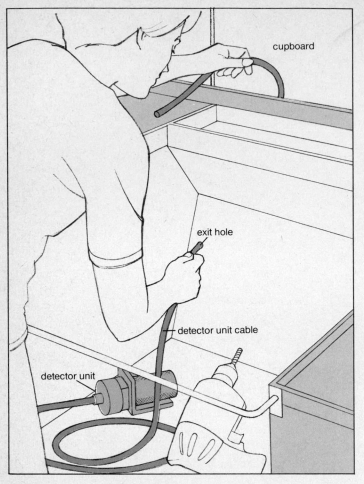

cupboard

exit hole

detector unit cable

detector unit

Put the detector unit on the mounting strap and adjust the cable so that there is sufficient slack to remove the detector for periodic testing. Install antichafing bushings in the exit hole and in the bulkhead hole to protect the cable insulation. Finally, seal the exit hole with bedding compound to prevent gas from escaping behind the stove recess. Seal any other open seams in the stove recess.

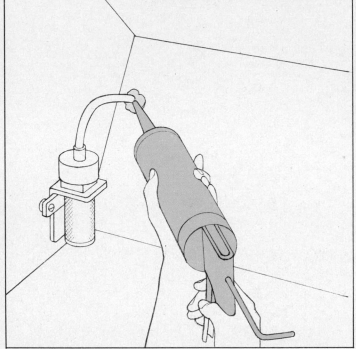

Next, run the detector unit cable from the stove recess to the bulkhead where the control panel will be installed. To do this, drill an exit hole in the rear bulkhead of the stove recess at right angles to, and a few inches higher than, the mounting strap. Thread the cable end through the hole and pull it up from behind the recess. In the typical situation above, a cupboard is above the stove; inside the cupboard, drill holes through the cupboard base and then the left wall, penetrating the bulkhead. Thread the cable up into the cupboard and then out the far side of the bulkhead.

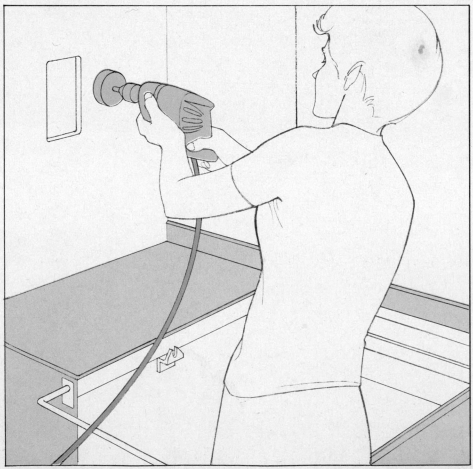

On the after bulkhead beside the stove, choose an easily visible position for the control unit and the meter. Make sure that there is space for the wiring on the other side of the bulkhead. Measure off and mark a rectangle large enough for the rear side of the control unit with its wire terminals. Drill a starter hole at each corner of the rectangle and cut out the rectangle with a saber saw. Alongside the rectangular hole, use an electric drill with a hole-saw attachment to make a circular cutout just large enough for the rear of the meter; with a rasp or rough file, smooth the holes cut in the bulkhead.

Position the control unit so that the plastic box is on the far side of the bulkhead, and the panel with its indicating lights lies flush against the bulkhead on the stove side. Mark the mounting holes. Drill pilot holes at the marks and secure the unit with screws or stove bolts. Repeat for the meter—placing it with its face on the stove side of the bulkhead and its cable dangling on the far side.

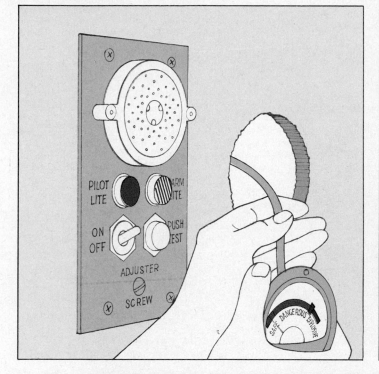

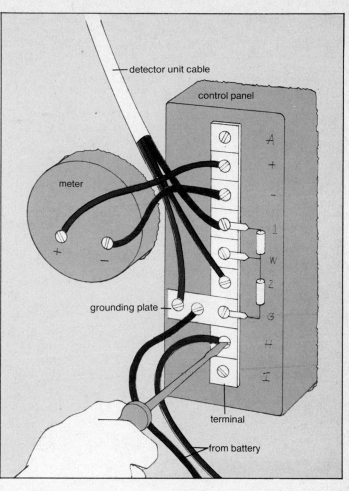

On the far side of the bulkhead of the stove, connect the two-wire cable from the meter and the three-wire cable from the detector unit to the terminals on the rear of the control unit, as shown above and in the wiring diagram on page 72. Finally, run a two-wire cable from the batteries to the terminals; connect the cable to the control unit terminals first, then to the battery terminals —being certain to turn off the battery switch before making the final connection, thus avoiding any risk of an electric shock.

Before replacing the stove on its gimbals, check the system. Turn on both the battery switch and the switch on the control panel, and allow the circuitry to warm up. Put a few drops of gasoline or lighter fluid in a can and cover it for about two minutes to allow the fluid to vaporize. Then place the detector in the can in a vertical position. Within 15 seconds, the red light and the horn should activate and the meter should register either "Danger" or "Explosive." Then wave the detector around in fresh air, and the alarm indicators should stop by themselves.

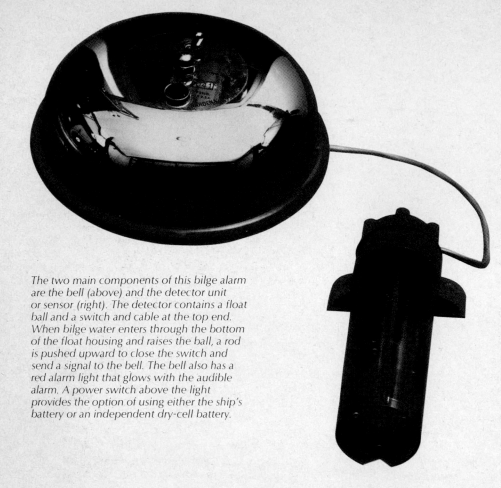

The two main components of this bilge alarm are the bell (above) and the detector unit or sensor (right). The detector contains a float ball and a switch and cable at the top end. When bilge water enters through the bottom of the float housing and raises the ball, a rod is pushed upward to close the switch and send a signal to the bell. The bell also has a red alarm light that glows with the audible alarm. A power switch above the light provides the option of using either the ship's battery or an independent dry-cell battery.

Bilge-Water Alarm

Next to an explosive fume alarm (pages 72-75), the most useful safety system a boatowner can install is a bilge-water alarm. If the boat springs a serious leak, a skipper on deck may not be aware of it until the water is over the floor boards. But an alarm can warn him to get the pumps going before either the engine or electrical system is flooded out.

In a bilge alarm like the one shown at left, a float-actuated detector switch activates an alarm bell. Extra bilge sensors can be added to most systems; in addition, the alarm bell also shown at left can be hooked up to various other types of sensor units—engine overheat detectors, fire detectors, and sensors to indicate low oil or water pressure.

The number and location of bilge units depends on the size and construction of the boat. If there are watertight bulkheads, a sensor should be mounted in each of the compartments. The first sensor should go in the engine compartment, where it should be mounted lower than the battery terminals or any rotating part of the engine. With planing hulls, one sensor should be located in the engine compartment and a second under the forward cabin sole, since bilge water will flow toward the transom when underway but will flow forward when the boat is at anchor. If the compartment is served by an automatic bilge pump, install the sensor level with the top of the pump. Thus if the pump has malfunctioned or cannot otherwise keep up with rising water, the bell will warn of the danger.

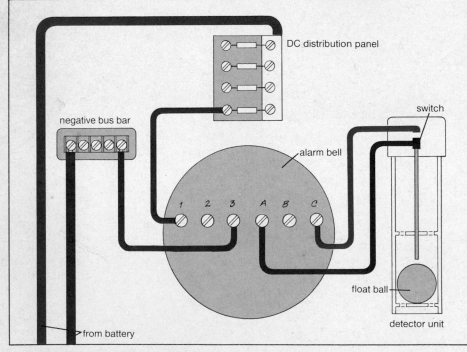

The wiring diagram for the bilge alarm shows that the two-wire cable from the detector is attached to the terminals marked A and C on the bell. The positive wire is run from terminal No. 1 to the DC distribution panel and the negative wire from terminal No. 3 to the negative bus bar. If a dry-cell battery is used, its positive feed is connected to terminal No. 2 and its negative to No. 3.

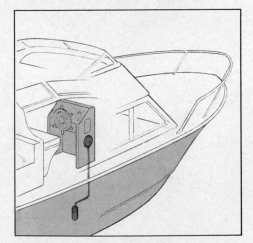

The detector unit of this bilge-water alarm is mounted at the lowest part of the hull, here under the cabin sole in the forward bilge. The alarm bell is on the side of the control console where it can be readily heard and seen by the skipper.

To install the detector, open a hatch in the cabin sole or raise a floor board over the keel. Measure from the lowest bilge point to the top of the floor beam. Estimate the safe limit to which bilge water can be allowed to rise. Adjust the detector unit to this level by aligning the center of the float ball with the appropriate inch mark on the ruler.

Hold the detector in place against the floor beam or other mounting surface and mark the position of the two screw holes in the mounting flange. Drill pilot holes at those points and fasten the unit with wood screws. Next strip a quarter inch of insulation from each of the wires in the detector unit cable and splice them to a cable long enough to reach the mounting position for the bell.

Cover the splices made in the previous step with electric tape and secure the wire to the floor beam with a plastic cable clamp. Then run the cable from the detector to the control console, keeping the cable as high as possible above the bilge-water level and securing it approximately every foot with plastic clamps.

Choose a spot out of the weather for the bilge-alarm bell; in the installation shown at right, the side of the control console provides a protected position that is also close to the power source (distribution panel, above) and to the electric bilge-pump switch (left of panel). To mount the bell, loosen the nut on the front (page 76) and remove the cover from the base. Place the base in the location chosen and mark the mounting holes at the top and bottom. Before drilling holes and fastening the base with wood screws, be sure that there are no wires or other obstructions on the other side of the console panel.

With the bell base in place, prepare to hook in the appropriate wires to their terminal. The holes above the numbered and lettered terminals mark the exact positions at which the power supply and detector unit wires must be led through for connection to the alarm bell. Use a small-diameter drill to make holes through the console side over the terminals marked No. 1, No. 2, A and C.

Pull the two wires of the detector unit cable (page 77) through the holes over terminals A and C; either wire can go to either terminal. Strip the end of each wire and crimp on a ring lug. Loosen the A and C terminal screws and fasten the detector unit wires in place. Next cut a length of wire long enough to reach from the bell to the distribution panel and another length long enough to extend from the bell to the negative bus bar. Pull the ends of these wires through the holes in the bell base and fasten the positive wire to terminal No. 1, the negative wire (here coded with white insulation) to terminal No. 3.

Locate on the distribution panel an unused circuit that can serve as a power source for the alarm system. Loosen the panel by unscrewing it from the console and locate the short black wire connected to the unused switch at the back side of the panel. Use a crimp connector in order to fasten the black wire to the other end of the wire from bell terminal No. 1.

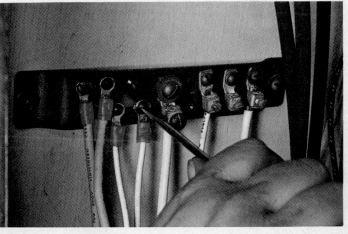

To complete the power connections, locate the boat's negative bus bar. This connection point for the negative wires from the electrical accessories is often mounted inside the control console and can be reached by removing the steering wheel and front panel from the console. Loosen a spare screw terminal and attach the other end of the wire from bell terminal No. 3 to the bus bar.

Screw the bell cover back onto the base, making sure that the toggle switch can be moved freely to both the "DRY" (for a dry-cell battery) and "SHIP" (for the ship's battery) positions. To make the system operational, set the bell switch to "SHIP" and make sure that the battery selector switch (page 68) and the appropriate distribution panel switch are turned on. Test the alarm by raising a coffee can full of water underneath the bilge-detector unit until the water reaches the mid-point of the float ball; at this point, the bell should ring. When the water level is lowered, the bell and light should turn off.

Running diagonally from upper right to lower left is the antenna of a VHF radiotelephone system. Emerging from the foot of the antenna is a transmitter cable, which is joined by a connector (bottom drawing) to a heavy-duty coaxial cable that will run down the inside of the mast. The other end of this cable is connected to another coaxial cable of smaller diameter. This will be led through the deck and along the overhead to another connector, which joins it to the radio's cable. From a socket at the lower right-hand corner of the radio a telephone wire leads to a wall-hung microphone.

Ship to Shore

Few shipboard accessories are more welcome than a VHF radiotelephone system. Such a system is composed of two major components: the radio itself, and the antenna. These are linked by two coaxial cables. One cable is heavy duty, about ⅜ inch in diameter, and on a sailboat must be long enough to pass through the mast from the top, where the antenna is mounted, to the bottom; on a powerboat the antenna is mounted on the side of the cabin deckhouse and the cable can be considerably shorter. The second cable is lighter in weight, about 3/16 inch in diameter, and long enough to reach from the foot of the mast, through the deck and to the companionway. The cables are joined to each other and to the antenna at one end, and to the radio at the other by a total of four coaxial cable connectors.

Despite variations in manufacturers' equipment, the same general principles apply in making any installation, as in the typical radio and antenna shown here and overleaf. Of major importance in the boatman's handiwork are the making of proper connections, snug fittings to guard against chafing, and the avoidance of sharp bends that will kink the wire—and interfere with transmission.

connector

microphone

smaller-diameter coaxial cable

connector

power cable

antenna

connector

mounting bracket

wide-diameter coaxial cable

antenna's transmission cable

connector

coupling ring   soldering holes   core conductor   copper mesh conductor

receptacle   plug assembly   adapter   insulation   coupling ring

vinyl jacket

This drawing shows the component parts of a coaxial cable connector. From right, a coaxial cable feeds into a coupling ring, then through an adapter (used only with a small-diameter coaxial cable, and omitted in the case of a large one), and into a plug assembly. After the cable's wires have been soldered to the assembly (opposite), the assembly tip snaps into a receptacle—a double-ended device that attaches to another coaxial cable, in mirror-image arrangement. When assembled, all parts screw together so that the coupling rings conceal the receptacle, the plug assembly and the adapter—if any.

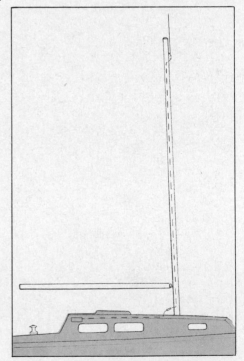

Mounted at the companionway of the boat, a VHF radiotelephone gives the skipper quick communication with shore and with other boats 50 miles and more away. The wiring for the apparatus goes from the radio, across the overhead, up through the deck and the inside of the mast to an antenna, which must be affixed to the masthead.

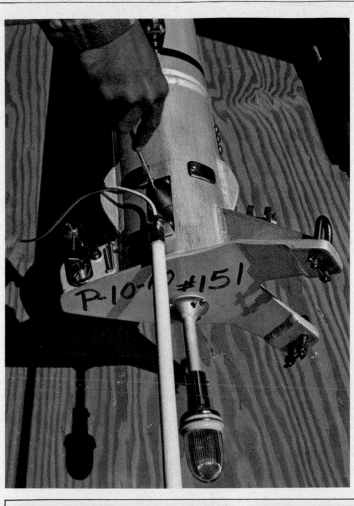

To mount a VHF radiotelephone aboard a sailboat, begin by unstepping the mast and attaching the antenna to the masthead. (In the photograph at left, the antenna's built-in transmitter cable is unconnected; it has not yet been affixed to the coaxial cable connectors.) Drill four holes in one side of the masthead and screw the antenna's mounting plate in place.

Drill two more holes, one about six inches below the antenna plate and another just above the foot of the mast. Feed an electrician's snake into the upper hole, down through the mast and out the lower one. Where the snake exits, fasten it onto the end of a large-diameter coaxial cable; then draw the cable up to the top of the mast and out the upper hole. Before attaching the cable to connectors (below), tape the cable about six inches from its end to keep it from slipping back down through the mast, and remove the snake.

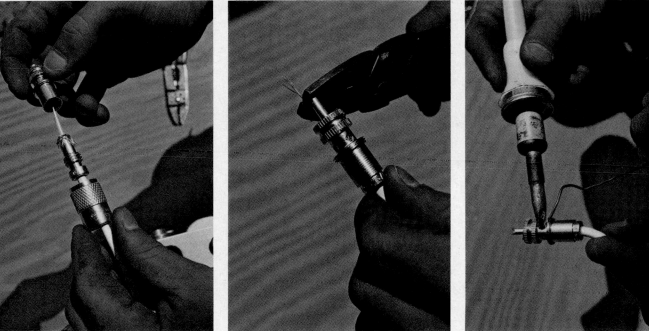

To install a small coaxial cable connector, strip the end of the cable's vinyl jacket, exposing ¾ inch of the copper mesh conductor. Strip the inner insulation to expose ½ inch of the core conductor. Slip on a coupling ring and an adapter. Fold the mesh back on the adapter and screw on the plug assembly (above, left). Nip off the ends of the core conductor (center) and solder at the tip of the plug; then solder the mesh through the soldering holes (right). Snap the plug into the receptacle and screw the coupling ring in place. For large cable do the same, but omit the adapter and do not fold back the mesh.

Just below the connector that joins the antenna's built-in transmitter cable, secure the large-diameter coaxial cable to the masthead by screwing a plastic bracket onto the antenna's mounting plate. This bracket will serve to prevent the cable from working in the wind and from chafing against the rim of the hole where it enters the mast for its descent to the deck.

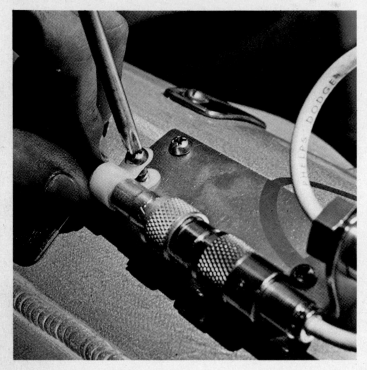

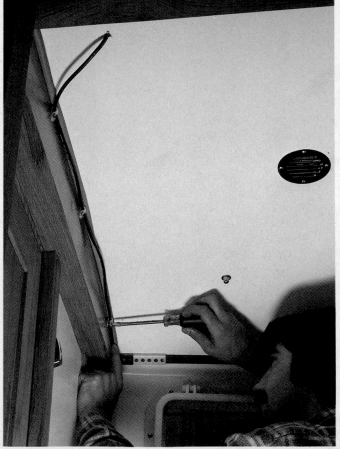

After the mast has been restepped and a connector fitted onto the large-diameter coaxial cable where it exits from the hole at the foot of the mast, drill a hole in the deck (upper right). Put a connector on the end of the small coaxial cable and join that connector to the large cable's connector. Slip a deck cable fitting (box, below) over the cable's unfinished end and then thread the cable end through the hole in the deck. Go below. Bring the small cable along the overhead, securing it in place as you go (lower right) until you reach the companionway bulkhead, where the radio will be located. Put a connector onto the end of the cable.

Watertight Entry for the Cable

The best way to lead a VHF cable through a deck is with the fitting shown here. It consists of a chrome-plated base, rubber gasket and screw-on chrome cap. First center the base over the hole for the cable and drill three small screw holes through it into the deck. Then slip the cable through the fitting and through the deck hole. When the cable has passed through, put bedding compound onto the bottom of the base and screw it onto the deck.

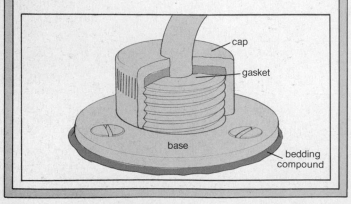

cap
gasket
base
bedding compound

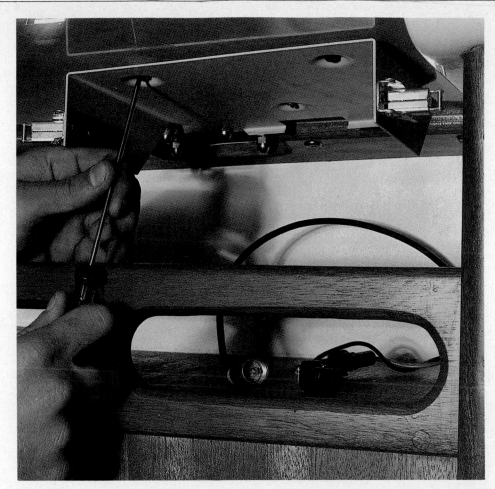

Drill holes into the overhead and screw the radio's mounting cradle in place (left). Then drill holes at a convenient location nearby and mount a bracket that will hold the radio's microphone.

Screw the small coaxial cable's connector onto the radio's coaxial antenna connector (built into the radio's rear panel), and lead the radio's power cable to the battery's service box. Place the radio in its cradle and snap the securing clamps shut (below).

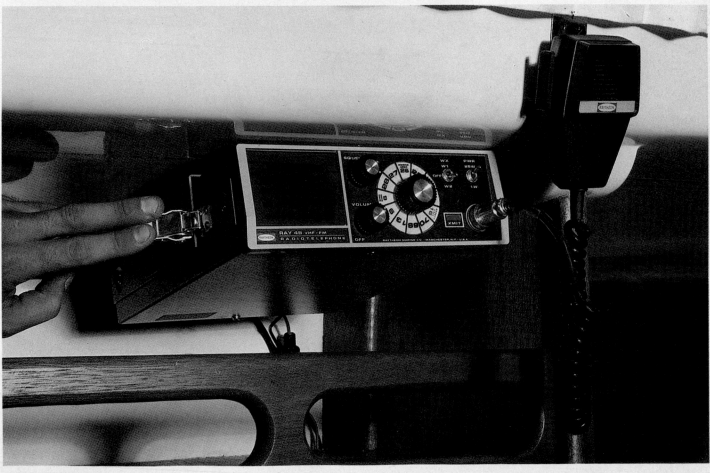

3 Most boats of any size are endowed by their builders with a basic plumbing system: a galley sink fed by a fresh-water tank, a marine toilet, a pump for emptying the bilges, and, on craft with inboard engines, the pipes to bring cooling water to the engine block or heat exchanger. To these essentials, the boatman can hook in any number of supplementary fixtures that will add to the safety and livability of his craft. The addition of a water heater, augmented by a small electric pump to pressurize his water system, will preclude the necessity of boiling up a kettle of water to wash the dishes or to shave. Any boat equipped with an electric bilge pump should be provided, for safety's

INSTALLING NEW PLUMBING

sake, with a manual backup. And to satisfy federal antipollution regulations, all old-fashioned marine toilets that are designed to flush directly over the side of the boat must be modified to prevent the dumping of waste material into United States waters.

All such alterations to a boat's basic plumbing have been greatly simplified by the advent of a variety of plastic hoses. Unlike copper pipe that must be soldered, or "sweated," in order to negotiate the twists and turns belowdecks, flexible plastic is easily manipulated through tight spaces and corners. It can be cut and trimmed with a penknife, and it can be attached effortlessly to threaded pipe, or to any piece of threaded plumbing equipment, by screwing on a plastic hose adapter. The hose slips over the adapter to be secured in place by a perforated metal clamp (or clamps)—which should always be stainless steel to avoid corrosion. Clamps are sufficient aboard ship because the pressure on any seagoing plumbing system is low—about 25 pounds per square inch, as opposed to double or more that in most households. The flexible hosing is available in various gauges—usually a light, transparent variety for fresh-water lines, and a heavy-duty opaque type for discharge pipes. The only instance where standard flexible hose is not recommended is in the installation of hot-water lines. Here rigid plastic pipe with a higher tolerance to heat should be used; instead of being clamped, the pipe is connected to its fittings with a special plastic solvent cement. And because plastic pipe is heavier than plastic hose, it must be cut with a hack saw, and the sawed edges trimmed with a knife.

Some plumbing jobs demand that the boatman hook into his craft's battery-powered DC electrical system. For example, to operate a pressure pump or a waste-treatment unit, wires must be run to the boat's DC service box. A hot-water heater requires shore power from a 110-volt AC dockside outlet—and as in all high-voltage installations, the final hookup of the heater to the boat's AC service box is best left to a professional electrician. In addition, since many plumbing fixtures, such as water tanks and sea cocks, are constructed of metal, they should be connected to the boat's electrical bonding system to prevent galvanic corrosion.

In making any of the improvements described on the subsequent pages, the implements found in most well-equipped tool boxes will suffice, with a few simple additions: a set of hole-saw blades for cutting through bulkheads, installing faucets and putting in through-hull fittings; a set of standard pipe wrenches; perhaps a basin wrench for tightening fittings where working space is scanty; and finally, an electrician's crimper for hooking up the wiring. And when adding any new plumbing device, remember that even the most careful installation will require periodic servicing and repair. It thus behooves the boatman to plan the location of each new fixture, wherever possible, in an uncluttered area where he can reach it later, and thus ensure its smooth and reliable functioning throughout each boating season.

A boatman tightens one of the nuts on a new sea cock in a fiberglass hull. A vital safety device for any hose near the waterline, the sea cock can be shut if a hose should rupture.

Layouts in Fixtures

The plumbing projects discussed on the following pages are shown here, newly installed on a sailboat and a power cruiser. The projects appear in blue, as do the water lines and electrical cables servicing them. The water heater on each boat requires an AC service box *(orange)*. The other plumbing projects that require electricity—the waste-treatment system and pressure pump on the cruiser—run off the boat's battery via the DC service box. The metal water tank and the sea cocks are wired to the bonding system *(green)*.

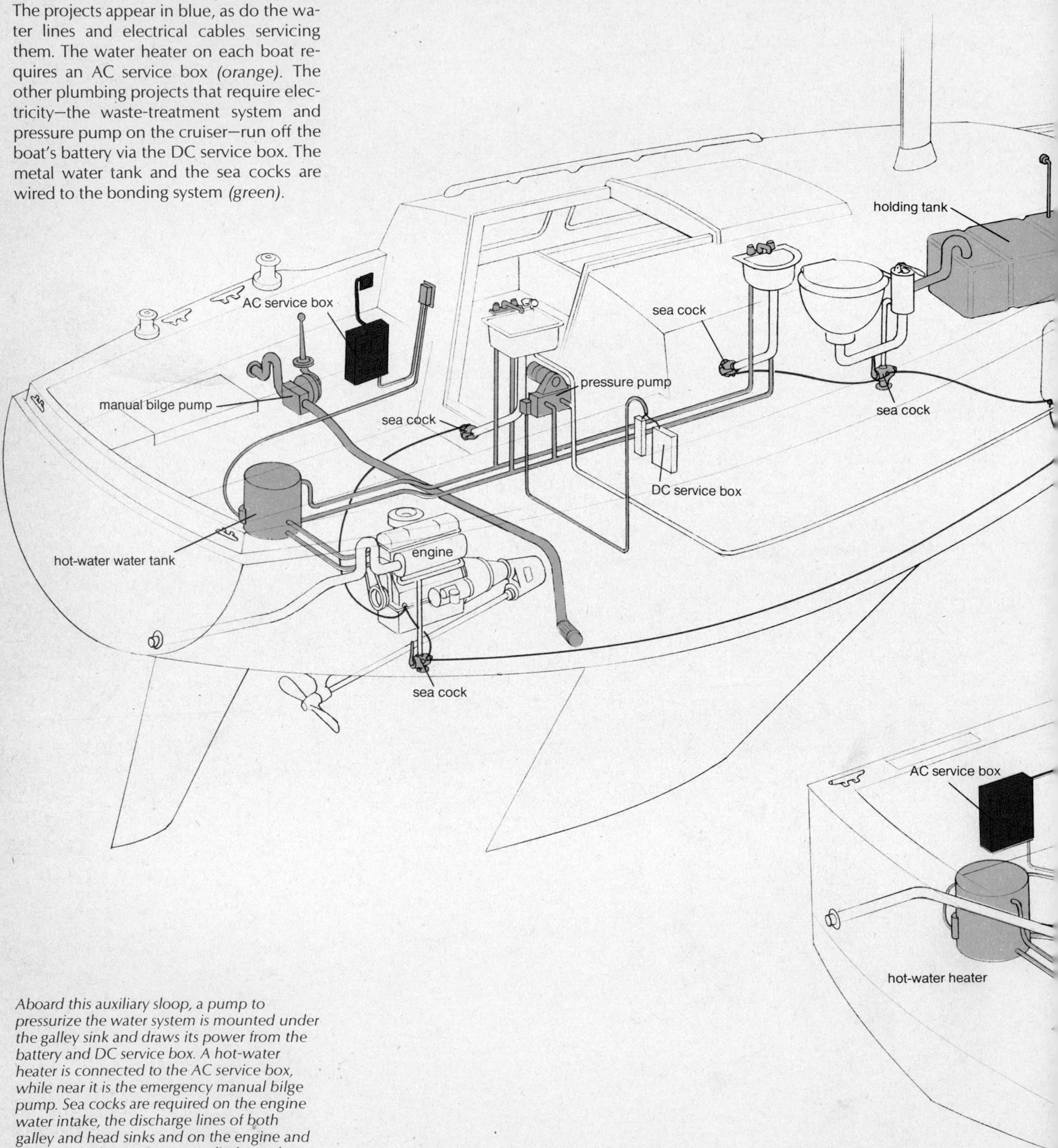

AC service box

holding tank

sea cock

manual bilge pump

pressure pump

sea cock

sea cock

DC service box

hot-water water tank

engine

sea cock

AC service box

hot-water heater

Aboard this auxiliary sloop, a pump to pressurize the water system is mounted under the galley sink and draws its power from the battery and DC service box. A hot-water heater is connected to the AC service box, while near it is the emergency manual bilge pump. Sea cocks are required on the engine water intake, the discharge lines of both galley and head sinks and on the engine and toilet intake hoses. For waste discharge from the toilet, the sloop has a holding tank tucked under a forward berth, its pump-out hose and vent leading topside.

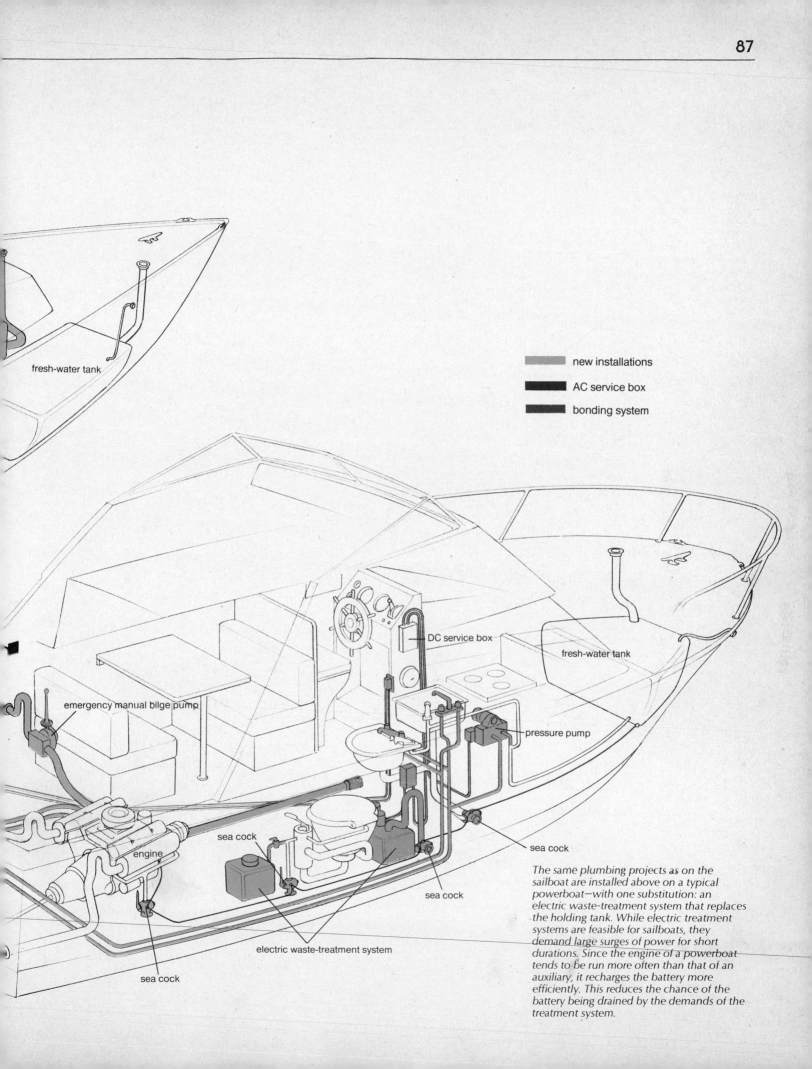

fresh-water tank

new installations

AC service box

bonding system

DC service box

fresh-water tank

emergency manual bilge pump

pressure pump

engine

sea cock

sea cock

sea cock

electric waste-treatment system

sea cock

The same plumbing projects as on the
sailboat are installed above on a typical
powerboat—with one substitution: an
electric waste-treatment system that replaces
the holding tank. While electric treatment
systems are feasible for sailboats, they
demand large surges of power for short
durations. Since the engine of a powerboat
tends to be run more often than that of an
auxiliary, it recharges the battery more
efficiently. This reduces the chance of the
battery being drained by the demands of the
treatment system.

Installing Sea Cocks

A sea cock controls the flow of water into or out of a boat through an opening in the hull near or below the waterline. The cock may admit raw water to cool an engine or flush a toilet, or, as shown below, may be part of a galley sink's drainage system.

Though installing a sea cock is a relatively straightforward job, a boatman who has never done it may worry about piercing his vessel's hull below the waterline. However, if he observes the precautions noted on these and the following pages, he will find that when he finishes, his hull is as sound and watertight as ever.

He first selects a sea cock, such as the heavy-duty bronze model at right, that can be attached to a wood, metal or fiberglass hull, and then considers exactly where to put it. The position should be readily accessible so that in an emergency the cock can be closed quickly, and so that it can be reached for maintenance lubrication every three months and for occasional checks to make sure that the valve has not frozen open or shut.

After fixing on a proper site, the boatman cuts a hole through the hull, makes a wooden backing plate and through-bolts the sea cock and the plate firmly to the inside of the hull. Next, from outside the hull, he attaches the through-hull fitting. He is then ready to screw on the tailpiece and couple to it whatever hose the sea cock will serve. Finally, he should connect the sea cock, like any other massive metal object aboard, to the boat's electrical bonding system.

A typical sea cock is a rotating valve set in a barrel housing and controlled by a handle. When the handle is vertical the valve admits water; when the handle is horizontal the valve is closed. The flange at the base of the sea cock is usually provided either with holes, as here, or notches for through-hull bolting; if the flange has neither holes nor notches, the boatman should have bolt holes drilled through the flange at a boatyard or a metal-working shop. A through-hull fitting screws into the base of the sea cock, and a tailpiece, to which a hose can be attached, screws onto a shank atop the sea cock.

handle

tailpiece

threaded shank

flange

bolt hole

through-hull fitting

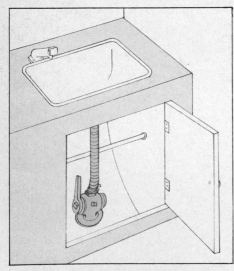

This sea cock, placed slightly below the waterline, drains water out of the galley sink. Since water that sloshes in from outside normally can rise only partway up the vertical drain hose, the sea cock is left open. However, in the event of a severe storm—or a hose rupture—the sea cock can be quickly shut in order to avoid shipping water.

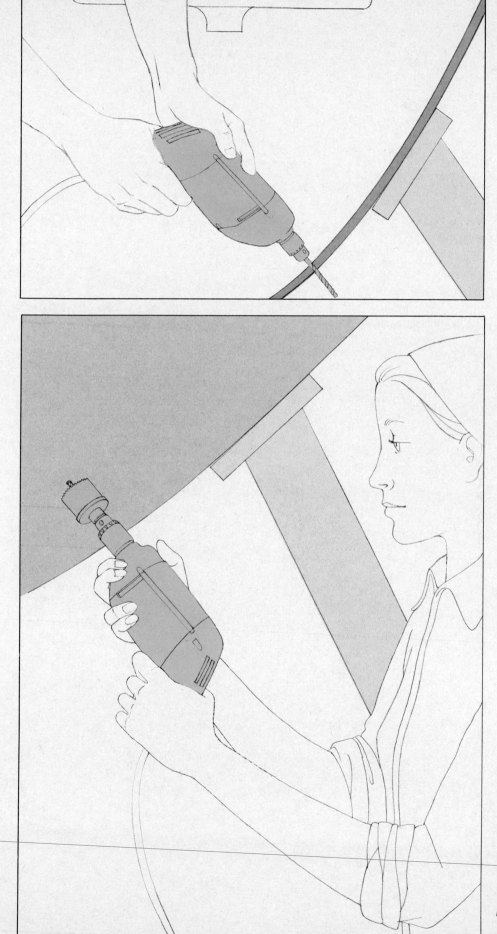

First set the sea cock on its base in the chosen spot—just below the waterline for a sink-drain sea cock or well below for one that must admit a constant flow of raw water, as for cooling an engine. Make sure there is room in this location for both the sea cock and the wooden backing plate (pages 90-91) on which it will sit, and that once installed, the cock will be easy to get at. Trace around the outside of the flange. Determine the center point inside this tracing and, from inside the hull, drill a pilot hole (left) through the hull.

Working from outside the hull, where there is more elbow room, attach a hole-saw bit to a drill. The blade's circumference should be slightly greater than that of the through-hull fitting. Insert the drill bit into the pilot hole (left) and cut most of the way through the hull. If possible, finish the job from inside the hull to prevent splintering around the perimeter of the hole. If the inside work area is too cramped, carefully complete the drilling from outside the hull.

To make the backing plate that will fit between the sea cock and the inside of the hull, first cut a hole the same size as the one in the hull through a piece of ¾-inch marine plywood. Center the sea cock on the hole and trace the outline of the flange onto the wood. Set the blade of a saber saw at an angle of about 45° and saw around the outline (right). The angled cut gives the plate a beveled edge from which water is inclined to roll away instead of settling and causing rot. As a further safeguard against damp rot, treat the finished plate with wood preservative.

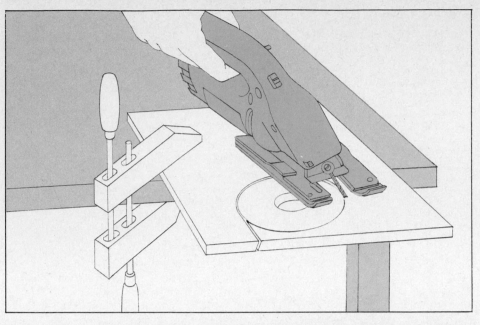

Liberally coat the bottom of the plywood plate with epoxy paste and press the plate firmly down over the hole. Seal the beveled edge of the plate with epoxy and make a watertight seam with more paste around its bottom edge. Wipe up any paste that has oozed into the hole. Spread bedding compound over the top of the plate and fix the sea cock in place on it by having a helper outside the boat screw the through-hull fitting several turns into the sea cock. With a bit of the same diameter as the bolts you will use, and with the flange holes as guides, drill bolt holes through the plate and hull (right).

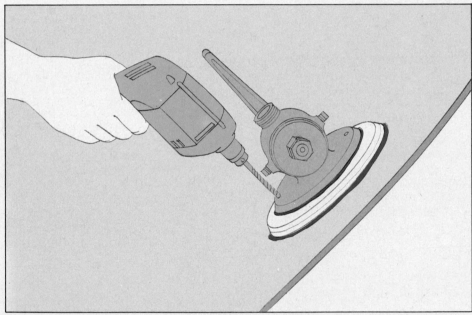

To make a watertight seal around the bolt heads, first countersink the bolt holes from outside the hull. Fill the countersunk holes with bedding compound, insert the bolts and tighten them from inside the hull. Remove the through-hull fitting. With a steel tape, measure between the hull's outer surface and the ridge around the inside of the sea cock (right). This distance, less ⅛ inch to ensure space between the ridge and the end of the through-hull fitting, is the fitting's maximum allowable length. If the fitting exceeds this length, trim it with a hack saw; a fitting that is shorter is usable just as it is.

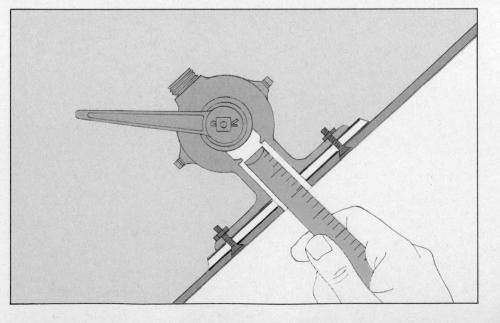

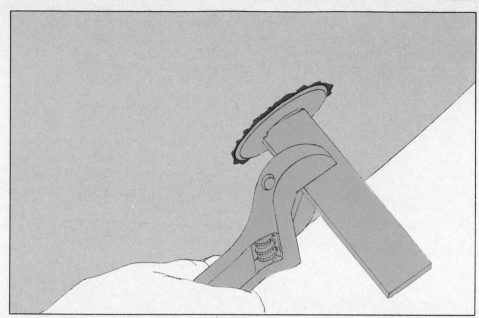

To install the through-hull fitting, first spread bedding compound on the inner side of the lip. Hand-tighten the fitting into the sea cock. Then insert into the fitting a piece of strap iron as wide as the inside diameter of the fitting. Brace the edges of the strap iron against the two small projections on the inside and near the mouth of the fitting. Grip the iron with a wrench and turn (left) until the increasing pressure has squeezed out most of the bedding compound. The fitting will then be about as tight as is necessary.

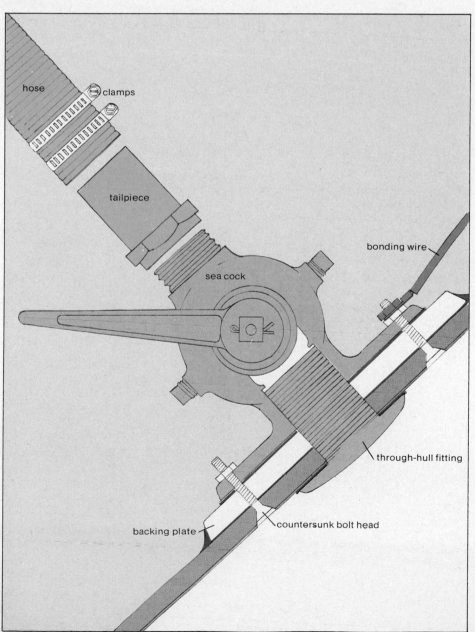

hose

clamps

tailpiece

sea cock

bonding wire

through-hull fitting

backing plate

countersunk bolt head

This cross section shows the sea cock through-bolted to the hull and backing plate, with the through-hull fitting in place. To complete the installation, screw on the tailpiece, slip the end of a hose over it and tighten the coupling with stainless-steel clamps. Finally, attach a wire to the threads of one bolt and secure it with a second nut, as shown. Connect this wire to the boat's bonding system—the wiring linking together and grounding all large metal objects to prevent the build-up of electrical imbalances that can promote galvanic corrosion.

This exploded view of the manual bilge pump shows the assembly of its rubber gasket and capped deck plate around the removable handle. Note that the pump's mounting bracket faces upward for installation beneath a cockpit seat, as detailed on the following pages. Some pumps, originally designed for floor mounting, come from the manufacturer with the bracket facing downward; they can be converted by detaching and inverting the handle socket on the pump's side.

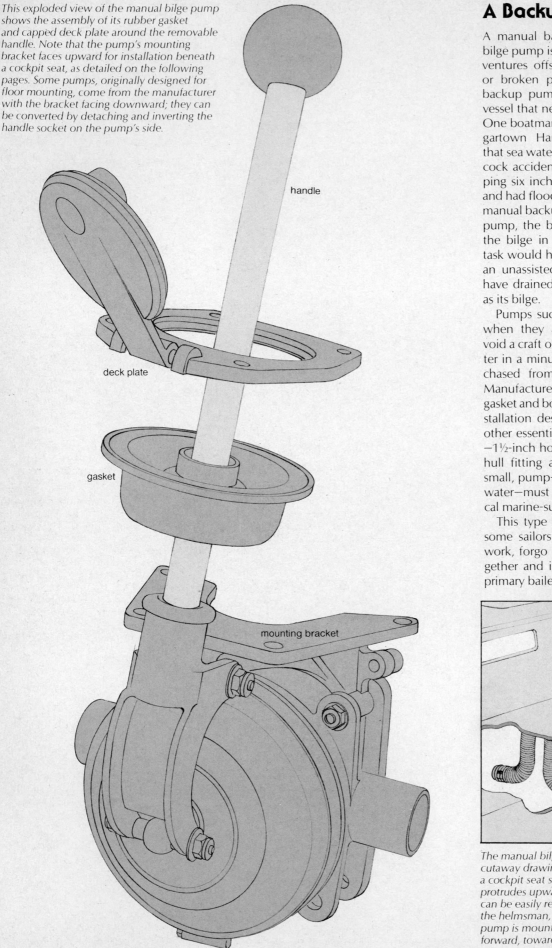

handle

deck plate

gasket

mounting bracket

A Backup Pump

A manual backup to a boat's electrical bilge pump is a necessity on any craft that ventures offshore, where an overloaded or broken pump can bring disaster. A backup pump can also be a boon on a vessel that never sails out of sight of land. One boatman returning to his craft in Edgartown Harbor, Massachusetts, found that sea water had siphoned through a sea cock accidentally left open and was lapping six inches deep over the cabin sole and had flooded out the engine. Using his manual backup in tandem with an electric pump, the boatowner was able to clear the bilge in only 45 minutes; the same task would have taken several hours with an unassisted electric pump and would have drained the boat's batteries as well as its bilge.

Pumps such as the one shown at left, when they are vigorously worked, can void a craft of more than 20 gallons of water in a minute. Such pumps can be purchased from a number of companies. Manufacturers also provide a deck plate, gasket and bolts that are needed for the installation described on these pages. The other essential equipment for the project —1½-inch hoses, hose clamps, a through-hull fitting and a strainer used to filter small, pump-clogging particles out of the water—must be bought separately at a local marine-supply store.

This type of pump is so efficient that some sailors, who don't mind the extra work, forgo an electric bilge pump altogether and install a manual one as their primary bailer.

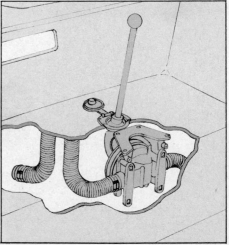

The manual bilge pump shown in this cutaway drawing has been mounted beneath a cockpit seat so that the pump handle protrudes upward. In this position the pump can be easily reached by a crewman or even the helmsman, if he is alone on deck. The pump is mounted so its intake nozzle points forward, toward the deepest part of the bilge.

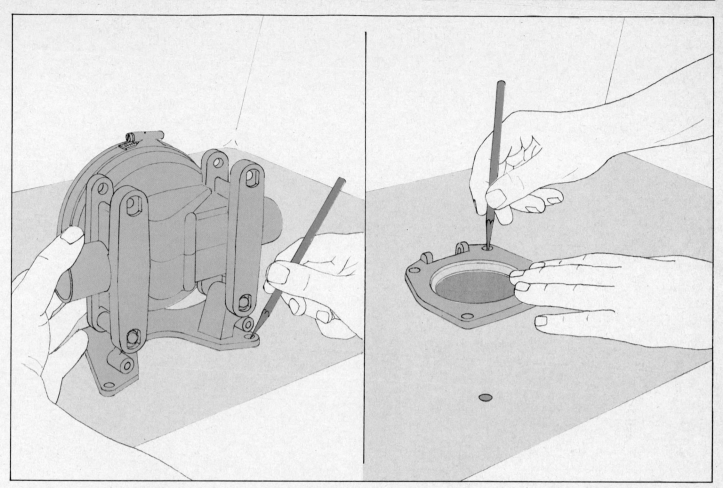

To position the pump and the deck plate's bolt holes in the cockpit seat, place the pump upside down on the seat top—in the exact mirror image of its intended installation below the seat (as shown above, left). Mark the pump's four bolt holes on the seat. Then line up the two inboard bolt holes in the deck plate over the two outboard holes for the pump; these two holes will be shared by the pump and the plate. Next, mark the deck plate's two outboard bolt holes (above, right). Finally, mark the position of the deck plate's hole on the seat.

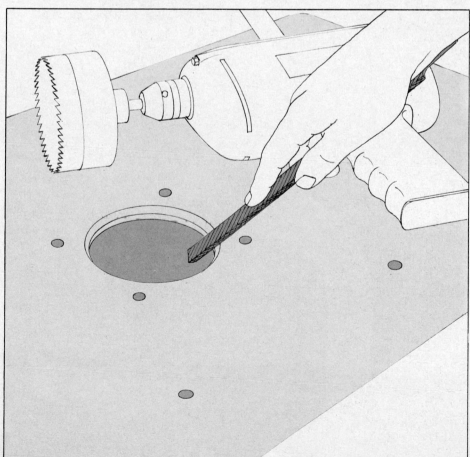

Drill the six bolt holes through the cockpit seat and cut out the handle hole with a hole saw. Then file the edges of the hole smooth so that they will not eat into the lip of the gasket that fits into the hole (overleaf).

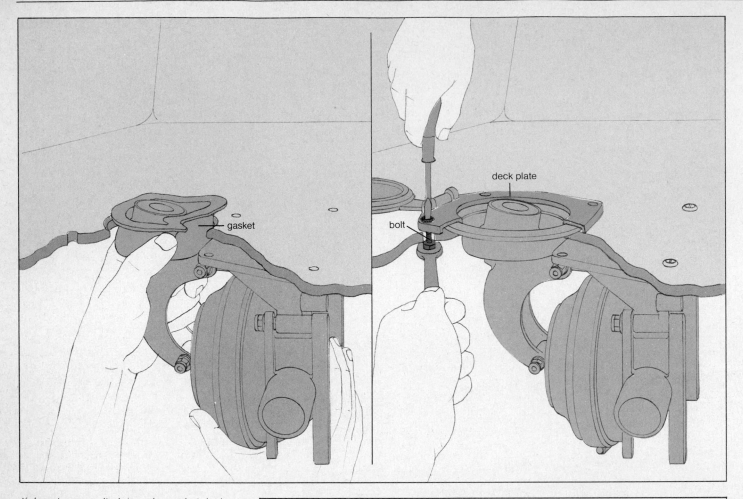

gasket

deck plate

bolt

If there is room, climb into the cockpit locker next to the bolt holes taking along the pump (seen here from forward), the gasket, six nuts and six washers for the mounting bolts. Slip the gasket over the pump handle socket. Then, holding the pump in position, squeeze the gasket so that it slips through the handle hole in the seat (above, left). A helper topside can then waterproof the deck plate and bolt holes with bedding compound and put the bolts through the holes. As the helper holds the bolts steady with a screwdriver, wrench them tight from below (above, right).

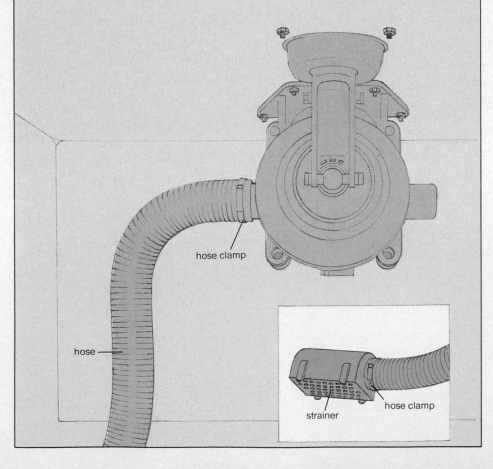

hose clamp

hose

strainer

hose clamp

After the pump (shown here in side view from outboard) has been bolted firmly in place, clamp a length of 1½-inch hose to the pump's intake nozzle with a hose clamp. The hose must be long enough to reach forward and down to the lowest part of the bilge—in most cases, just forward of the auxiliary engine. To the bilge end of the hose, clamp a strainer (inset) that will prevent particles from lodging themselves in the hose or pump.

Next install a through-hull fitting (left) at least 10 inches above the waterline, if possible. Cut the hole in the hull with a hole saw and waterproof the through-hull fitting with bedding compound. A cutaway of the fitting and its mounting nut is shown below. Clamp a hose to the pump, loop it up to the seat, fasten it, then clamp it to the fitting.

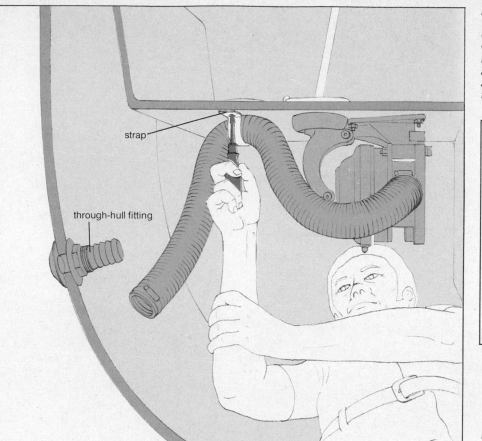

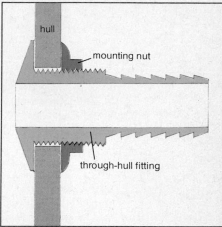

With the assembly completed, the intake hose sucks in water when the handle is pumped topside. The water flows through the pump, up into the loop—which prevents backwash through the outlet hose—and out of the boat via the through-hull fitting.

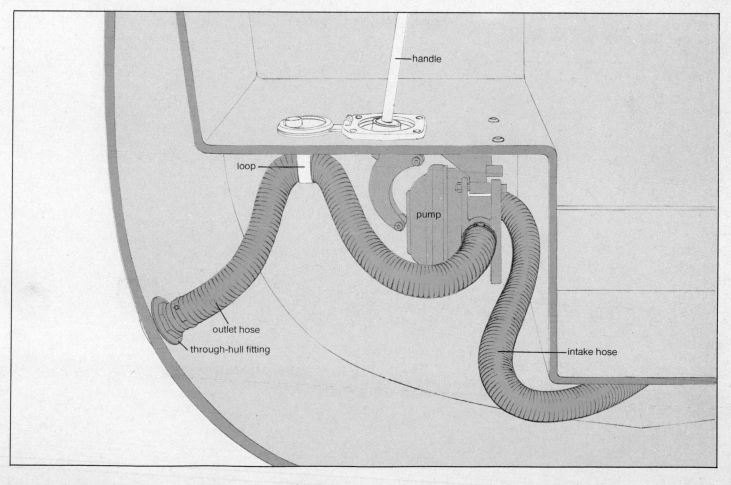

A Holding Tank

The simplest way to satisfy federal and state laws forbidding the flushing of toilets directly overboard is to install a holding tank. Two types of holding tanks best fit into the limited space aboard most boats. One is a heavy-duty flexible plastic bag that slips into any area no matter how awkward. The other is a rigid plastic tank, similar to a gasoline tank, that can be fitted into an unoccupied storage compartment close to the head, such as under the V berth in a sailboat, as shown here.

To put in the rigid tank, the boatman lashes it firmly in place with tie-down straps, then hooks up three flexible plastic hoses that service it. One hose brings waste from the toilet. Another goes to a deck plate to allow the tank to be pumped out at a marina. The third is a vent that runs to a through-hull fitting placed well above the waterline. The vent permits fresh air to circulate in the tank to dissipate the accumulated gases; it also prevents a vacuum from forming when the tank is being pumped out.

The hoses should be of heavy-duty plastic so that they will not collapse under the pressure of pumping. The vent and pump-out lines can be run directly from the holding tank to their hull and deck fittings, but this means exposing the unsightly hoses in the forward cabin. To avoid this, pass the hoses through the bulkhead so that they are seen only in the head.

With the tank hooked up, the old overboard discharge hose, with which boats have been customarily equipped, can be removed and the sea cock sealed up.

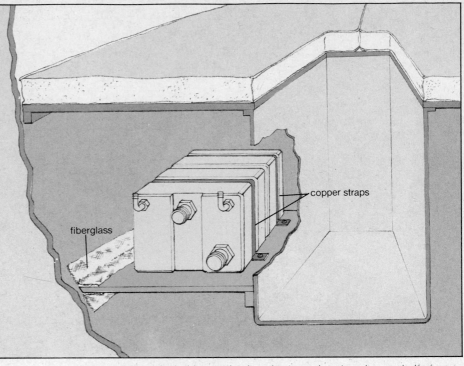

To give the holding tank a firm, horizontal resting place, a shelf of marine plywood at least three quarters of an inch thick should be built to hold it. Mold the outboard side of the shelf to the hull with fiberglass (pages 20-21), and screw down the shelf's inboard side to a length of lumber that is glued and screwed to the wooden berth riser. Line up the tank fore and aft, so the fittings for the hoses face the toilet. Then secure the tank in position with heavy transverse nylon or copper straps attached to the plywood with screws and washers.

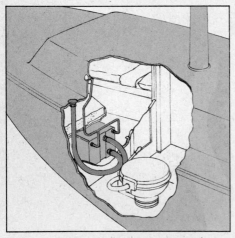

There are several reasons for installing the holding tank in a sailboat under the V berth forward of the toilet. The bulkhead keeps the tank hidden; the space is usually roomy enough for easy installation; and it is accessible for periodic readings of the level of the liquid.

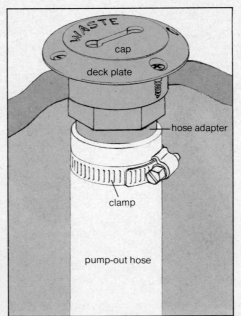

To install a deck plate for the pump-out hose, cut a hole in the deck the same diameter as the lower section of the plate. Put bedding compound on the plate's lip, fit the plate into the hole and screw it in place. From belowdecks, screw the hose adapter into the plate. Cut a hole through the bulkhead so the pump-out hose can pass from the tank into the head and up to the deck plate.

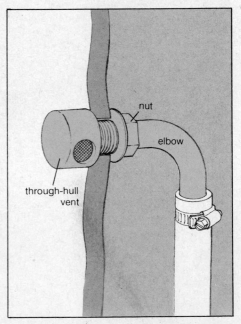

The hole for the tank's vent can be drilled either in the cabin housing, as seen here, or directly into the topsides. Keep the hole as high as possible above the waterline. Apply bedding compound to the elbow and insert it in the hole; then, from belowdecks, tighten the nut that holds the fitting in place. Drill a hole through the bulkhead to allow the vent hose to pass from the tank to the fitting.

vented loop

discharge sea cock

To hook up the toilet to the holding tank, first disconnect the discharge hose from the vented loop of the original overboard flush system; the loop, designed to prevent sea water from siphoning back into the head, can now be removed. Cut a hole through the bulkhead, lead the discharge hose through and clamp it to the tank's intake connection. To seal off the discharge sea cock, screw a brass pipe cap onto the threaded shank on top of the fitting—an easier task than removing the sea cock and patching the hole.

The completed job is shown in the drawing below with the toilet hooked up to the holding tank, all hoses in proper position, and the discharge sea cock capped. Any spaces between the hoses and their holes in the bulkhead can be filled with bedding compound. An unusual feature of this particular holding tank is its twin vents, which lead to a single vent hose. The two-vent tank is designed especially for sailboats. When the boat heels on either tack, one of the vents will always be open.

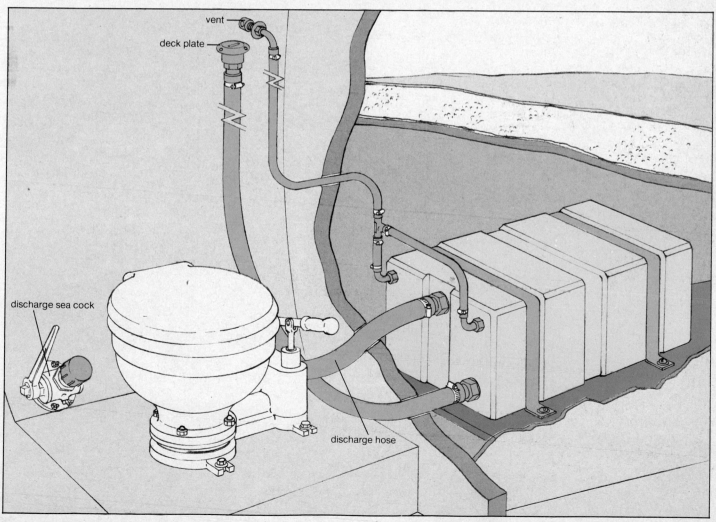

vent

deck plate

discharge sea cock

discharge hose

A Waste-Disposal Unit

For areas where local regulations permit the disposal of treated waste, this miniature on-board system provides efficient, automated, odor-free treatment and does not require the stowage, handling, or use of chemicals. It may be used with almost all types of marine heads, whether they are operated manually or electrically.

The machine treats waste inside a dual-chambered, thick-walled plastic tank that is connected into the waste line of the boat between the toilet and the discharge sea cock. A charge from the boat's 12-volt electrical system reacts inside the tank with the salt in the sea water being used for flushing. The hypochlorous acid that is produced disinfects and deodorizes the waste, which is then pumped overboard. The entire process takes only 2½ minutes and is regulated by a single control unit. When the boat is operating in fresh or brackish waters, the necessary salt is supplied from an auxiliary tank connected to the toilet.

The installation of this three-unit system—including the auxiliary salt tank—is relatively simple but requires some advance preparation. For example, once the arrangement of the units has been determined, wooden frames must be built to fit around the bottoms of the treatment and auxiliary salt tanks—as shown on the opposite page—to hold them securely in their chosen locations. If the space selected for the treatment tank is going to be too cramped for the boatman to work in comfortably after the unit has been put in place, basic fittings should be attached to it ahead of time.

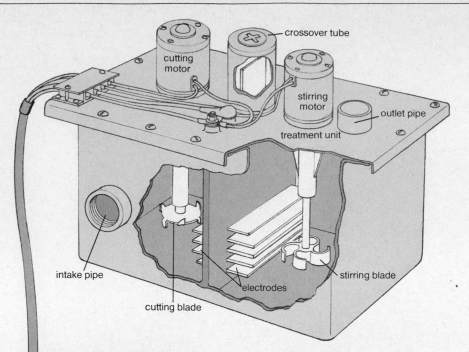

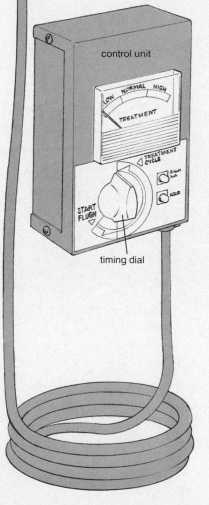

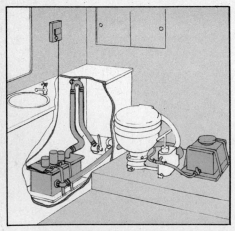

All three units of this electrolytic disposal system should fit conveniently inside the boat's head. The controls are on a nearby bulkhead, the auxiliary salt tank is beside the toilet, and the treatment tank is concealed inside a cabinet; alternatively, the latter might go beneath the cabin sole or under a bunk in the next cabin.

The major components of the waste-disposal system are activated by rotating a timing dial on the control unit (left) and immediately flushing the toilet. Waste enters the treatment unit (above) through its intake and is broken down by motorized blades. Passing through a crossover tube into a second chamber, it is kept suspended by stirring blades. Meanwhile, electrodes in both tanks react with the salt in the water to disinfect the material, which is then discharged through the outlet. A needle on the control unit indicates the concentration of salt in the treatment unit.

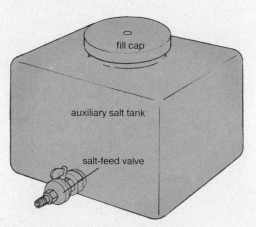

The two-gallon auxiliary salt tank holds a solution of water mixed with five pounds of ordinary table salt, which is fed into the toilet. In fresh water, the salt-feed valve should be opened all the way; for brackish water, three fourths of the way. The valve may need to be adjusted for each flush until the control unit's needle reads normal—to show that adequate treatment is taking place.

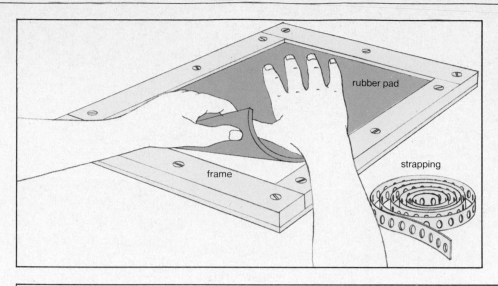

The mounting frame for the treatment tank (and salt tank, if one is needed) should be of one-by-two-inch wood strips with a ¼-inch marine plywood base. Measure the wood strips to fit around the base of the tank. Scribe the plywood base to the tank's dimensions and add a margin for the one-by-two-inch strips. Cut the base; glue and screw the strips in place. Cut ⅛-inch-thick rubber padding to the inner dimensions of the frame; lay it in place. Cut two lengths of metal strapping to wrap snugly around the tank, protecting the corners with rubber pads; screw to the sides of the frame (below).

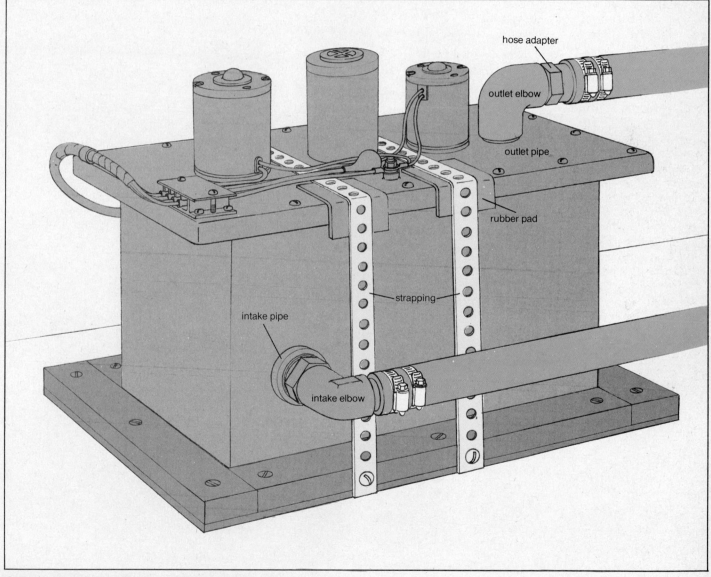

Once the treatment unit has been strapped down, the entire assembly is secured to the cabinet floor with screws. If the work space is too cramped, the screw holes for the frame should be pre-drilled. The plumbing connections for the treatment unit begin at the outlet pipe where the outlet elbow is rotated into position and glued in place with plastic solvent cement. A hose adapter is then screwed into the free end of the outlet elbow. Finally, the intake elbow screws into the intake pipe, and hoses are secured at both elbows with double clamps.

To connect the auxiliary salt tank, first close the sea cock to the toilet's outside water intake and disconnect the intake hose (below) at the pump. In its place (right), clamp on a short piece of hose; into the hose put the stem of a T-check valve fitting. Finally, clamp the end of the intake hose over the larger arm of the T-check valve, and clamp the salt-feed line over its smaller arm.

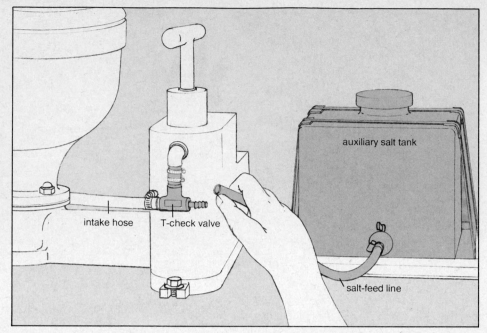

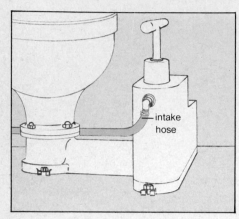

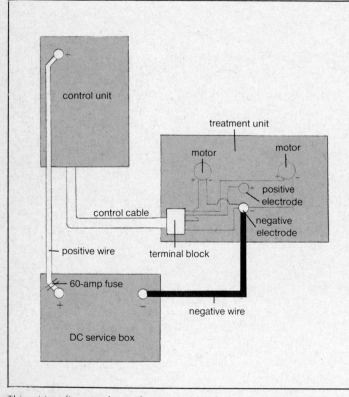

This wiring diagram shows the circuitry for the waste-disposal system. A positive wire (white) leads from the DC service box to the control unit; this positive linkage should be protected at the service box with a 60-amp fuse. A 12-foot control cable brings four wires from the control unit to the terminal block on the treatment unit. Positive connections from these wires run from the terminal block to the unit's motors and positive electrode, and finally from the motors to the negative electrode contact, from which a single negative wire (black) returns to the DC service box, completing the circuit.

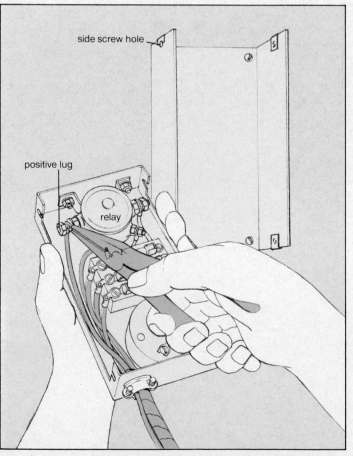

Unscrew the control unit and mount the empty housing to the bulkhead with wood screws. Attach the four wires of the control cable to their proper terminals in the control unit. Hook up a positive wire to the positive lug on the control's relay. Last, place the wired unit into the mounted housing and secure with its side screws.

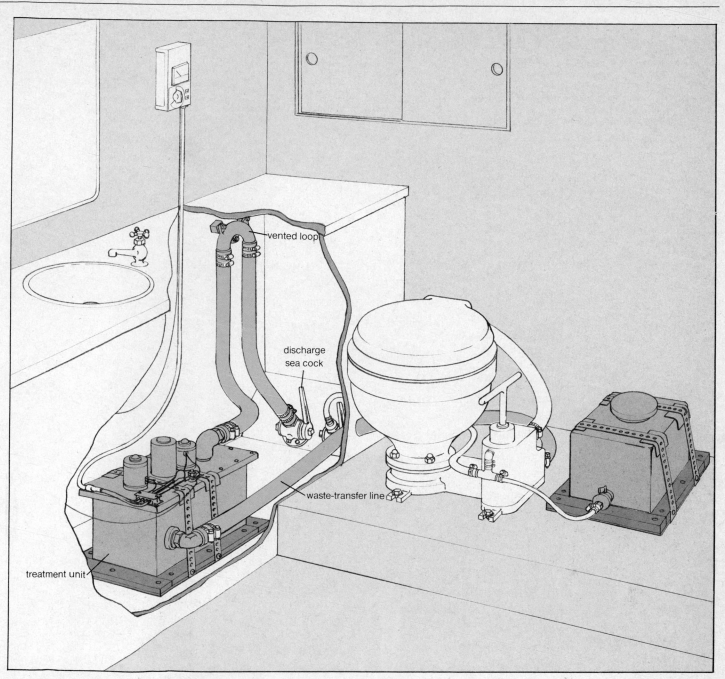

vented loop

discharge
sea cock

waste-transfer line

treatment unit

The treatment unit rests at or below the level of the toilet bowl in
order to prevent backflow, and is connected to the toilet by a 1½-inch
neoprene or plastic waste-transfer line. If the hose must be bent
around a sharp corner, the boatman can use an auto radiator hose
with the curve already molded in. The hose between the treatment
unit outlet and the discharge sea cock should include a vented loop,
as shown here, if the treatment unit is near or below the waterline.

Running Water

A welcome addition to any boat is a pressurized fresh-water system that eliminates the inconvenience of hand pumps in galley and head sinks. The system requires the installation of a lightweight electric pump, new faucets and a few sections of flexible plastic hose.

The heart of the pressure system is the electric pump, which draws water from the boat's storage tank and sends it to the galley and head sinks. The pump saves electricity by going into action only when water is needed.

For maximum water pressure throughout the system, the pump should be installed as close to the boat's water tank as possible. If sufficient space is not available there, a suitable alternative is to install the pump in the cabinet under the galley sink, as shown here and on the following pages.

In order to provide a stable base for the pump and also to conserve space under the sink, a wooden bracket must be built for mounting on the bulkhead. This job is made easier if the bracket is placed on a part of the bulkhead that has an exterior surface accessible for drilling and screwing (overleaf). Before fastening the pump and bracket to the bulkhead, the boatman adds a new faucet to the galley sink —though he keeps the existing hand pump as a backup. On the head sink, where there is less space, a faucet takes the place of the hand pump.

Compact and quiet, this electrical pressure pump weighs about eight pounds and rests on rubber pads that absorb vibration. When an open faucet lowers the pressure in the water system, a vertically moving diaphragm in the pump sucks water from the storage tank through the intake valve and forces it into the pipes via the discharge valve.

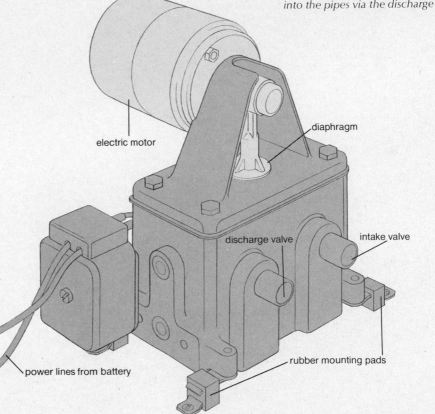

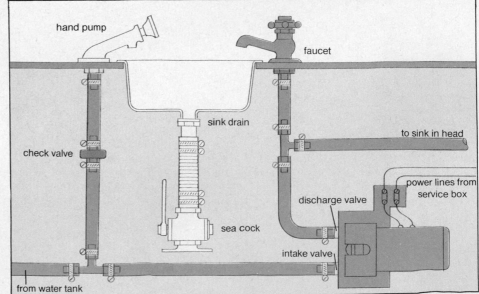

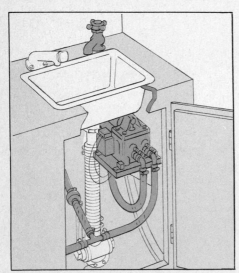

The cabinet under the galley sink usually offers enough room for a water-pressure pump and its accompanying plastic hoses. The cabinet door can be closed to muffle what little noise the pump's electric motor makes. And, with the pump perched on a wooden bracket above the cabin sole, there is still stowage room below it for such galley essentials as soaps and scrub brushes.

This is a schematic view of a fresh-water system with an electrical pressure pump, a new faucet, and plastic hoses installed under the galley sink. The hand pump is left in place as a reserve water source, its feeder line fitted with a check valve. The pressure pump pulls water from the tank and pushes it to the new faucet; along the way, a T connection diverts some of the flow to the sink in the head. Power lines from the boat's DC service box provide electric current for the pump. The sink drains overboard through a sea cock.

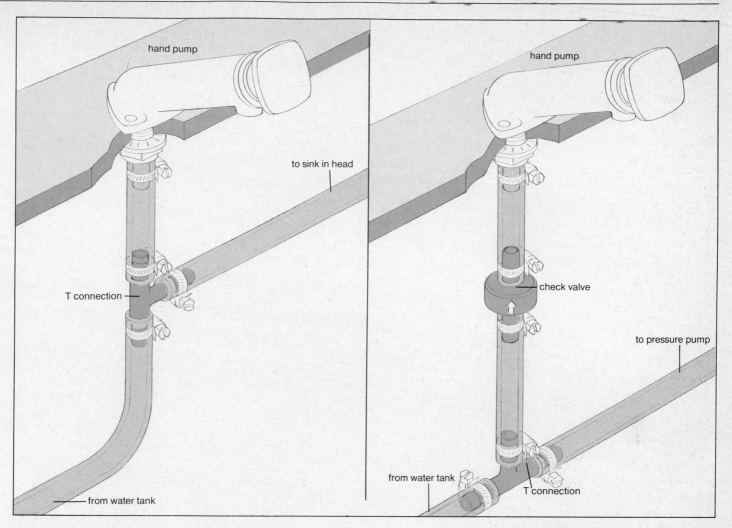

hand pump

hand pump

to sink in head

T connection

from water tank

check valve

to pressure pump

from water tank

T connection

To convert a hand pump in the galley sink to a standby water source, some minor plumbing adjustments are made, as shown in the two drawings above. At left is the hand pump before the conversion, its feeder line interrupted by a T connection that allows water to flow to the sink in the head. At right, the T connection has been removed and repositioned between the water-tank line and the new pressure pump. In its place on the feeder line is a check valve that permits water to pass up to the hand pump but keeps air from leaking back into the system and dissipating the water pressure.

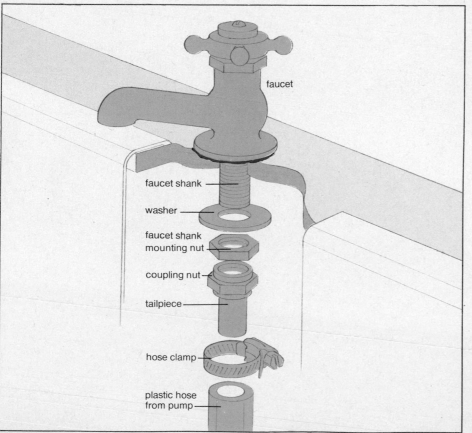

faucet

faucet shank

washer

faucet shank mounting nut

coupling nut

tailpiece

hose clamp

plastic hose from pump

The parts needed for putting a new faucet into a galley sink are arrayed here. Begin the job by drilling a hole the diameter of the faucet shank in the sink's counter. Run a bead of bedding compound around the base of the faucet and slip the faucet into the hole. From under the counter, place the washer on the faucet shank, then screw on the mounting nut and tighten it with a wrench. Next, screw the coupling nut of the tailpiece onto the shank. After the pump is in its permanent position on the bulkhead (pages 104-105), attach the hose to the tailpiece with a clamp.

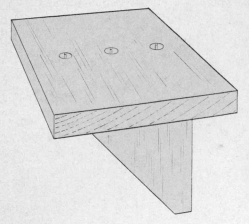

The bracket that holds the pressure pump on the bulkhead is made from two ¾-inch-thick pieces of hardwood. One is a rectangular shelf slightly larger than the pump base. The other is a triangular brace that is attached under the shelf by three screws.

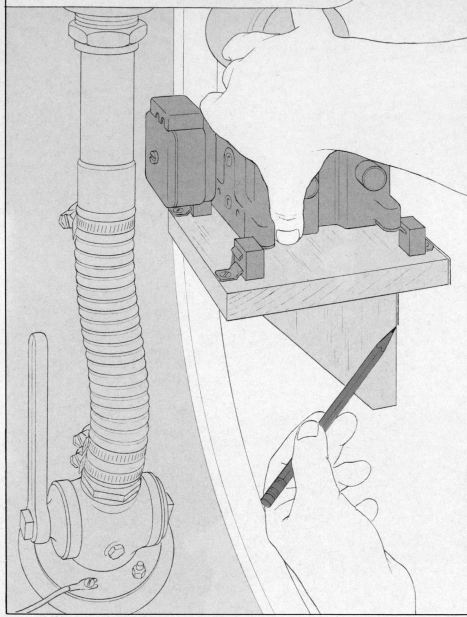

After the pump has been screwed onto the bracket, hold the assembly under the galley sink to find its best permanent location. Place the bracket as high off the sole as possible to leave space below for storage, but be sure the pump does not hit the bottom of the sink. When the proper position is selected, inscribe a line, as shown, on the bulkhead around the perimeters of the bracket.

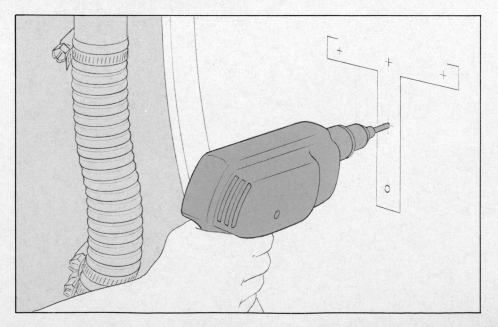

Within the outline drawn on the bulkhead, mark five points to drill holes for the screws that will hold the bracket. Drill the holes all the way through the bulkhead. Next, take the drill to the other side of the bulkhead. While an assistant holds the bracket in place on the outline, drill back through the holes with a smaller bit; this back-drilling will leave screw holes in the bracket. With the assistant still holding the bracket firmly against the bulkhead, insert and tighten down the screws.

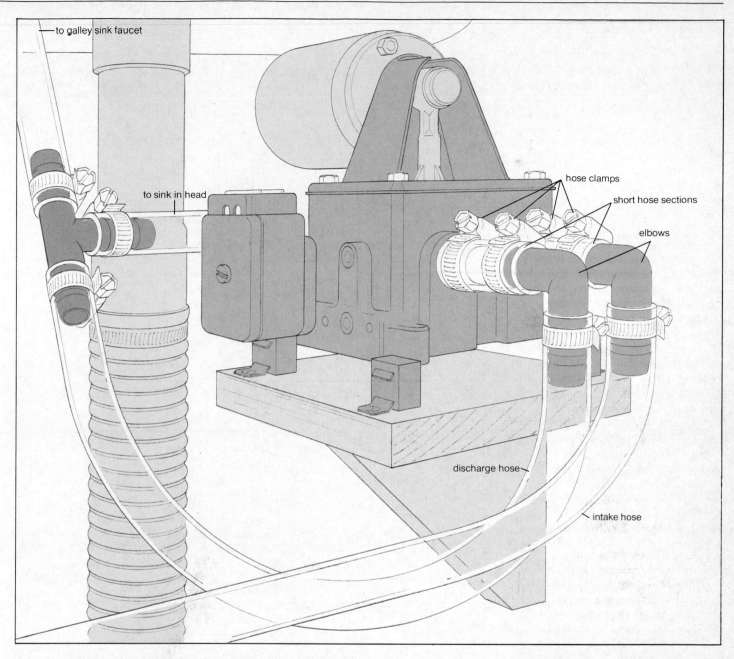

to galley sink faucet

to sink in head

hose clamps

short hose sections

elbows

discharge hose

intake hose

Once the pump is in place, its plastic hoses are attached, using plastic elbows at the intake and discharge connections. To install these elbows, clamp sections of hose about three inches long onto the connections. Slip the plastic elbows into these sections and secure each with a clamp. Attach the hoses to the elbows. Attach the discharge hose to a T connection. Link a hose from the T connection to the tailpiece of the faucet.

The concluding step in the installation is to screw the positive and negative wires from the service box to the pump's electrical connection box. Make sure the electric terminals are clean and dry. Then turn on the faucet to start up the pump, and check carefully for any leaks.

4 Beyond the 10 or so basic knots, splices, bends and hitches that every boatman must know, there are an almost infinite number of additional rope forms, decorative and utilitarian, which he can master to improve both the beauty and function of his vessel. The multiple half hitches being bent onto the steering wheel in the photograph at left, for example, appear to be designed just for decoration; actually, they serve the eminently practical function of giving the skipper a firm grip on the helm. The Portuguese bowline *(overleaf)* was designed long ago for straightforward utility, yet like all of the other ropework shown on subsequent pages, it has a handsome and seamanly look to it.

ROPEWORK PLAIN AND FANCY

In addition to the useful and esthetic virtues of these knots, the tying of them is itself a satisfying pastime, a kind of maritime sculpture that quickly takes form under the hands and eyes of the boatman. That is one reason why sailors since ancient times have occupied themselves with this practice; the crews of sailing ships used to while away the long sea voyages by trying to outdo one another in knotsmanship.

All these knots have a long history. In fact, some have outlived their initial purpose and survive today in an entirely new guise. The tack knot *(pages 120-121)*, for instance, was once used on windjammers to secure the tack, or forward edge, of a sail. Today, though, metal fittings have taken over the function of securing the tack; but the tack knot is still being tied—usually as a decorative fillip for the end of a bell rope or grab line. One old seaman's yarn tells of an English tar named Matthew Walker who was condemned to death, then offered a pardon on condition that he tie a knot that the judge —himself a former seaman—would not be able to undo. The sailor disappeared into his cell with 10 fathoms of rope and devised, exactly in the middle of the line, the deceptive knot that today bears his name. He then reemerged to present his invention to the judge. The judge was stumped, and Matthew Walker received his pardon as promised.

This story conveys a number of enduring truths about knots. One is that in the sailor's world, a knot exists for every conceivable purpose—including saving the life of a condemned man. Another is that the vast majority of knots in the nautical spectrum, though they may at first appear incomprehensible even to a fairly well educated eye, are easy and relatively quick to tie once the boatman learns how. The knot that confounded the judge, for example, can be fashioned within about two minutes—though nowadays it is generally made near the end of a line rather than in the middle—by anyone who knows the trick *(pages 120-121)* of unlaying the strands before he starts. Several of the other knots on these pages are, like the Matthew Walker, started by unlaying the line and reworking the separate strands. Others, among them the intricate-looking monkey's fist *(pages 114-115)*, are tied with the end of the line remaining intact.

Different kinds of rope have special qualities that suit them to certain kinds of knots. The easiest material to use is cotton; it can be manipulated comfortably—without chafing fingertips or splitting nails, which prickly manila has a tendency to do—and it serves well for knife lanyards and ditty bags. However, cotton is neither strong nor durable and should never be used for working lines. For heavy-duty apparatus, such as sheets, halyards, anchor lines or a water-ski rig *(pages 44-45)*, modern synthetics such as nylon and Dacron are best; they neither shrink nor rot after having been soaked in water. And for good, workaday versatility, many boatmen feel that nothing beats manila; it makes a sturdy knot whose sculptural outlines clearly show, and has an old-fashioned look that warms the hearts of tradition-minded seamen.

A handy sailor provides a better grip on the wheel of her coursing auxiliary by laying on a series of half hitches—called French spiral hitching—that turn a ridge around the rim.

The Portuguese Bowline

One of the handiest of the specialized knots is a double-looped bowline called the Portuguese bend, which makes an excellent emergency bosun's chair for hoisting a person aloft to repair a mast. Its two interconnected loops can be adjusted after the knot is formed, so that one loop will fit around the person's chest and the other will make a sufficiently roomy seat. If it is properly tied, the knot will support the heaviest person aboard without either slipping or jamming.

To tie a Portuguese bowline, coil a pair of counterclockwise turns into a piece of line. Hold the coils securely with the left hand, and with the right hand grasp the point at which the line's working end crosses over the standing part, as shown. Then turn the right hand palm upward (white arrow), so that the working end passes first down behind the coils and then up through them.

Continue turning the right hand until the working end has been brought completely up through the two coils, and lies parallel with the standing part. You will have now created a small loop in the standing part, with the working end running up through it, as here.

The Jug Sling

The jug sling is a special-purpose knot that originated ashore as a makeshift horse bridle, but has found particular usefulness in provisioning or unloading a boat. Drawn up tight around the mouth of a large water bottle, it forms a pair of reliable rope handles for hauling bulky liquid containers from shore to ship or vice versa.

The first step in tying a jug sling is to make a simple noose. This is most quickly done by fashioning an overhand knot with a bight from the standing part pulled through the turn, as above. Do not pull the overhand knot tight, and be sure the noose formed is a foot or more in diameter.

Make a secondary round turn within the noose by twisting its end so that one part of the line lies above the other, as shown above. Make this turn large enough so that you are able to bring it down and entirely encircle the loosely tied overhand knot (arrow).

Leading the working end of the line behind the standing part, then forward, bring it down over the two coils and back again through the small loop.

Grasp the working end and the right side of the inner coil in the right hand, and the standing part with the left, and pull in the direction of the arrows to draw the knot tight.

With the Portuguese bowline completed, its two continuous loops can be adjusted to any combination of sizes; and when a strain—like the weight of a man—goes onto the knot, neither of the loops will slip.

Now bring the bight of the original noose carefully over the enlarged round turn; then turn it downward toward you and weave it under the overhand knot (arrow).

Draw the knot tight by grasping the loop of the noose in one hand, and the standing part and working end in the other; pull slowly and carefully in the direction of the arrows.

Cut the standing part of the line at a point equal to the remaining length of the working end. Then tie the two ends together with a square knot to form a loop equal in size to the loop from the noose. The two loops become the handle of the jug sling, while the strands in the center cinch tight in order to grasp the mouth of the bottle.

The Monkey's Fist

Besides being a highly ornamental knot, the monkey's fist serves the very practical purpose of weighting the end of a heaving line. The knot consists of three sets of interlocking round turns, with four turns in each set. When the knot has been completed—but not yet pulled tight—a small weight such as a lead ball, a stone or a golf ball is inserted into the middle. After being pulled tight, the fist can be finished off simply by splicing the leftover working end into the standing part. In this way, the fist becomes a permanent part of the heaving line.

Less conventional—but far more useful—is the finishing technique shown here, in which one turn from the monkey's fist is extended and then seized into a permanent loop. The monkey's fist can then be bent onto any heaving line as needed.

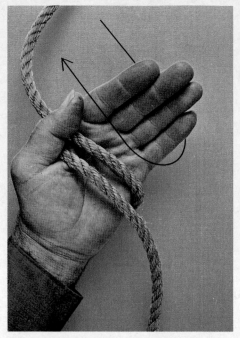

Begin work on the monkey's fist by laying the line across the palm of the left hand so that about 10 inches remain as the standing part. Secure the standing part with the base of your thumb; make a total of four turns with the working part around the hand in the direction of the arrow. This completes the first set of turns for the monkey's fist.

To start the second set, ease the first set down toward the fingertips, still gripping the turns with the thumb. The working end is now ready to be turned (arrow) around the first set and at right angles to it.

Tuck the standing end (arrow) into the knot, thus creating a fourth turn on the side of the first set that had only three; now the monkey's fist is symmetrical, and the essential structure of the knot complete.

With your fingers, pry open a section of the knot at a junction of two rings; slip in the weight you have chosen—here a golf ball wrapped in twine for extra heft and bulk.

Start at either end of the line and tighten the knot around its heavy core. Use a marlinespike, as shown, advancing the slack (seen here looping upward) as you go. Work through the knot's entire structure again until you reach the third or middle turn of the five-part ring. Here, reserve enough slack—about 18 inches—to form a loop; keep tightening the knot on the other side of the loop.

Grip the first of these turns for the second set with the thumb and forefinger. Wrap (arrow) the working end around the first set until there are four turns in the second set.

Now start the third set by tucking the working end through the first set of turns, as shown. Take care that the same tension has been kept on the line through each turn of each set so far, so that the knot retains a symmetrical shape.

To complete the third and final set of turns, rotate the left hand so the turns of the second set are vertical. Bring the working end up through the horizontal turns of the first set, next to the fingers. (This will add a fifth turn to the second set.) Cross the working end over the vertical turns outside them; again thread it through the horizontal turns (arrow). Repeat until you have four turns.

Inspect the knot for tautness and firmness on all sides and, if necessary, work the turns again, adjusting the length of the loop handle until it approximates that shown above.

Cut off all excess line flush with the outside of the knot. The ends need not be whipped to prevent fraying; with use they will work back inside the knot altogether.

Finish the monkey's fist by wrapping a seizing for about an inch around the throat of the loop handle. This will prevent any part of the loop from working its way back into the knot and thus loosening it.

The Turk's Head

The elegant Turk's head makes a fine handgrip on the end of a tiller or on the top spoke of a ship's wheel. It can also be used as a ring for snubbing up the draw-strings of a duffel or ditty bag *(pages 134-137)*. A small one may even be laid flat to form a coaster on shipboard; a larger one can become a place mat.

Depending upon the purpose it is to serve and upon the diligence of the rope-worker, a Turk's head is structured of two or more parallel lines, or leads, worked into three or more bights or interweaving sections. A particularly popular form of the knot, with three leads and five bights, is shown here. Whatever the size, all Turk's heads are worked in the same way —a continuous under-over pattern executed one complete circle at a time.

To tie a Turk's head, lay the standing part of the line across the inside of the left hand so that the standing part—or bitter end—is down and the working part leads up and away from you. Wrap the working part around the hand and back across the first turn with the working part hanging behind, as shown.

Carry the working part up and over the first turn and weave it under the bight at right. Pull the entire length of the working end through the bight—as you will do in all subsequent weaving steps.

Inspect the knot at this point to see that each section of the knot is locked together by the interweaving of lines under or over each succeeding bight or turn, as shown. The basic construction of the Turk's head is now set.

Rotate the hand back to its palm-inward position. Start the second round in forming the knot by bringing the working end up under the line on the left side of the palm. Here, and in all subsequent steps, the working end as it comes through should lie to the right of the lead that it runs beside.

Turn the hand to the palm-outward position and continue to follow the lead established in the previous step, going under and over accordingly and always staying parallel and to the right of the lead.

Now rotate the hand so that the palm faces out and the two turns of line run parallel across the backs of the fingers. Raise up the turn on the left and cross it over (arrow) the one on the right, as shown.

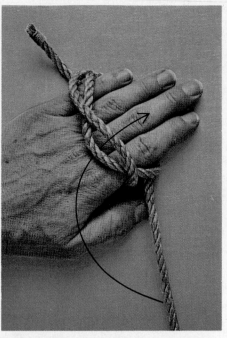

Bring the working end up and, approaching from the wrist side of the hand and going toward the fingers, weave it under the bight that is now on the left over the one on the right (arrow).

Weave the working end in the opposite direction (arrow), going under the turn on the right atop the little finger. Be sure to keep the knot very loose at this stage as you will need room to maneuver in later steps.

When all parts of the knot have been doubled, as shown, begin the third circuit of the Turk's head. The pattern of placement remains the same, parallel and to the right of the leading line.

The weaving of the knot is completed when each of the five bights or turns consists of three parallel sections of line. Now tighten the knot, either on itself or on the spoke or post for which it is intended. Start at the working end and follow that single line toward the other end, pulling it snug, until you have circuited the knot three times.

To dispose of the two projecting ends, pull firmly on one of them and whip the extended end close to the knot. Now, cut off the line just beyond the whipping. Repeat the process with the other end and tuck both behind the interwoven bights. The finished knot now appears to have no beginning or end.

The Wall Knot

The wall knot is the basic building block for a series of more elaborate stopper knots and splices *(overleaf)*. It is the simplest of multistrand knots—those formed by unlaying a line and tying its strands. To make it, each strand in turn is passed *up* through a bight formed by the adjacent strand, as shown in the diagram below.

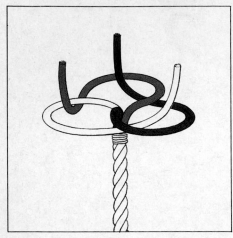

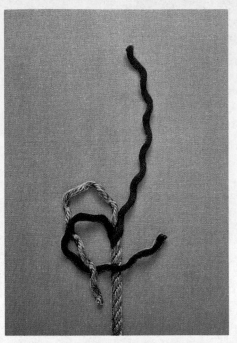

To start a wall, unlay about eight inches of line and hold the line in one hand with the strands pointing upward. With the other hand, turn the strand at the left (red, above) down toward you in a counterclockwise direction to form a bight, placing the end of the strand in front of the line's standing part.

Now turn the middle strand (colorless) counterclockwise through the bight of the first strand, forming a second bight identical with the first.

The Crown Knot

The crown knot, the reverse of the wall knot *(above)*, is often put on top of a wall; together they form an excellent stopper knot. The crown is formed by pulling each strand *down* through the bight of the next strand, and ends with the strands pointing downward. The crown is also used by itself to start a backsplice, or with a series of crowns to make a decorative braidwork called a crown sennit.

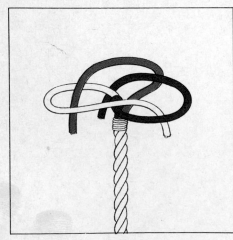

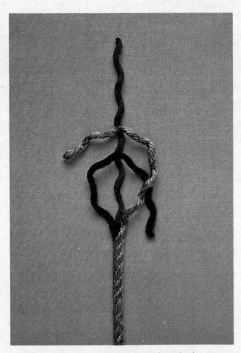

To make a crown alone, unlay the line and bring the left-hand strand (red) clockwise across the center strand (yellow) and down under the right-hand strand (colorless).

Now pass the right-hand strand (colorless) counterclockwise over the center strand (yellow), making a second bight similar to the first one.

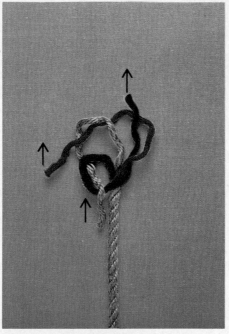

Pass the third strand (yellow) counterclockwise through the bight of the second strand (colorless), forming a third bight. Finally, tuck the first strand up through this bight, as shown by the arrow.

Tug the strands—one by one, and little by little—in an upward direction (arrows), slowly drawing the knot together and working it into its finished shape.

When pulled tight, the completed knot encircles the end of the standing part in three symmetrical bights. All three strands now point upward, ready to begin a new knot.

Holding the second bight in place, begin the third bight (yellow) by looping the center strand counterclockwise and passing it down through the bight formed by the first (red) strand, as shown by the arrow.

With the final strand now caught under the bight that was formed by the first strand in the initial step, the knot is ready to be drawn into its final shape.

Work all three strands downward, slowly and carefully, tugging on them one at a time —firmly but not too hard—until the crown is closed tight.

The Tack Knot

The tack knot is a multistrand knob fashioned at the end of a line, where it makes a decorative and permanent terminal for a bell pull, a bucket lanyard or a handhold at the end of a strap hung next to the companionway ladder. The knot is built up by first tying a wall, then superimposing a crown, and finally leading each strand back through the knot to double both the wall and the crown. An old sailors' ditty describes the process: "First a wall, then a crown; Now tuck up, then tuck down."

Each of the steps shown at right should be done with the knot kept fairly loose, so that the strands can be woven through easily when doubling. Even so, a marlinespike will be necessary for the last series of tucks, in which the strands are led down through the knot's center, parallel with the standing part.

Lay open the rope for about 12 inches, and whip the throat and the ends of the strands. Make a wall knot, and then fashion a crown (preceding pages) directly on top of the wall. Leave each knot fairly loose. Then take one strand (red) and tuck it back up through the knot (arrow), following the lead of the nearest strand in the wall knot; the new tuck will lie below the old lead and parallel to it.

Continue doubling the wall knot, tucking each strand in turn, in each case following below and parallel to the original lead. Thus, in this example, the red strand will follow the red lead, and the yellow strand the yellow lead. End with the strands pointing upward; prepare to make the first tuck for doubling the crown (arrow).

The Matthew Walker

Another handsome terminal knot with much the same uses as the tack knot is the Matthew Walker. One of the oldest of multistrand knots—mention of it appears in British admiralty records as early as 1644—it was utilized in old sailing ships as a stopper knot to keep a line from reeving out through a deadeye. Today it adds a distinctive element to any number of ropeworking projects, such as making a lanyard or a ditty bag like the ones shown on pages 132-137.

Lay open about 12 inches of rope; whip the throat and the end of each strand to avoid fraying. Arrange the strands in crescents going counterclockwise. Bring the left-hand strand (red) around the standing part and pull it through its own bight, forming an overhand knot. Then prepare to make a similar overhand knot around the standing part with the center strand.

Bring the center strand forward over the tip of the first strand, below the first bight and around the standing part. It will form its own bight; lead the end back up through this bight and the previous one for the second overhand knot. Repeat with the third strand (yellow), leading the end through its own bight and the two previous ones for a third overhand knot around the standing part.

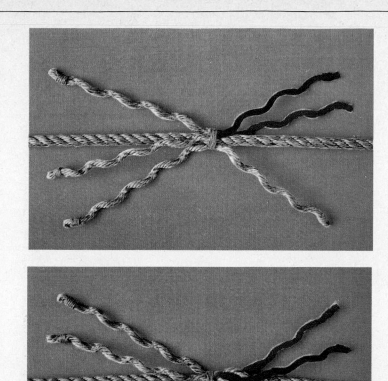

The Short Splice

The short splice is a stout way of permanently joining two lines of equal material and diameter, and thus lengthening dock lines, towing lines, anchor rodes and the like. However, the splice forms a bulge that is double the rope's normal diameter, so should never be used for lines that are intended to run through a block or eye.

To make a short splice, unlay the strands of two line ends for six to eight inches. Interlace the three strands from one line with the three strands of the other, as shown, so each strand lies between two of the opposite line. This is called "marrying" the two lines. Put a temporary seizing around the marry where the six strands come together.

After you have married the two lines, take any loose strand (in the picture at left, the red one) from the left-hand line, pass it over the nearest strand of the right-hand line, then tuck it under the strand—going against the lay as in the back splice (opposite). Give both of the lines a one-third turn away from you and proceed in the same manner with the next loose strand (yellow) and finally with the third (uncolored) strand. Take three complete tucks in all.

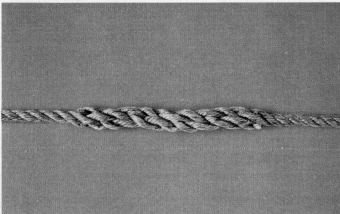

Cut off the seizing and flip the rope so that the part in which the three tucks have been taken now lies to the left. Pull the remaining three loose strands tight and work them, one at a time, through the rope as before—each strand going against the lay, first over and then under a standing strand. Make three complete tucks.

Cut the ends off all six strands, leaving about ¾ inch protruding. Roll the splice between the palms of your hands or underfoot until the protruding strand ends have been pressed into the splice and are no longer visible. The two lines have now been joined into one, and are ready for use.

The Long Splice

The long splice joins two lengths of line so smoothly that the splice will run through a block or any other type of fair-lead. Essentially the simplest of all splices to execute, it is weaker than a short splice, but has the advantage of not significantly increasing the diameter of the lines at the point where the two are laid together.

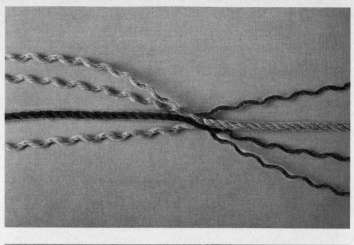

To make a long splice, unlay two ropes at least 15 inches for each half inch of the lines' circumference. Then marry the strands (right top), joining the two unlaid lines together, end to end, so that the strands of one pass between the strands of the other.

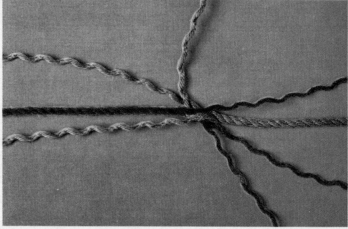

At the marry, take any two corresponding strands—say, the center strand of each line (here, the left-hand line and its strands are tinted brown for easy identification)—and tie an overhand knot. Leave the knot just loose enough to be readjusted later during splicing.

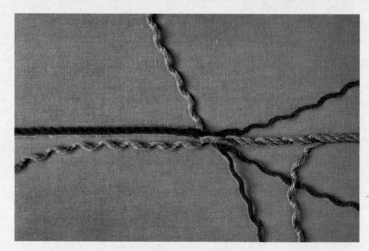

Take one of the unknotted strands (shown untinted at right) and unlay it away from the marry; here the chosen strand has been unlaid back down the right-hand line. For clarity and simplicity, the strand at right has been unlaid only a few turns; in making a serviceable splice, however, the strand should be unlaid some 10 or 12 inches for each half inch of the rope's circumference.

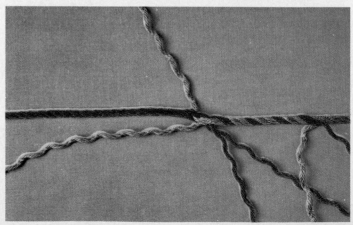

Now take from the left-hand line the strand corresponding to the one just unlaid, and lay it into the spiraled groove left open by the unlaying. Stop when you reach the end of the groove, and the two strands meet; both should have bitter ends of three or four inches.

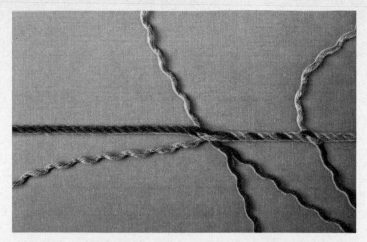

Where the newly laid strand meets its counterpart, make an overhand knot and pull it tight. Then go back to the crotch, smoothing the new-laid strand in its groove as you go, and pull the crotch knot tight. Make sure that both knots have equal tension, and that the tension is sufficient to snug the strands down into the line but not enough to cause bunching or an uneven lay anywhere on the line.

From the left-hand line, unlay the remaining unknotted strand another 10 or 12 inches for each half inch of the rope's circumference and, in the groove it leaves, lay in its counterpart from the right. Where the two strands meet, tie another overhand knot and pull it tight.

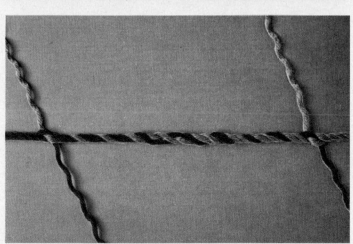

Make sure that all laid and re-laid strands have equal tension. Then return to the crotch and the first knot you tied. Take two snug tucks with each of its loose strands, working each one over, then under, then over and under again, the strand nearest to it in the standing part of the rope. Snip off the ends, leaving a quarter of an inch.

Take two tucks with each dangling strand at both ends of the splice and snip each end off a quarter of an inch from the rope. Then roll the rope between your palms or underfoot, smoothing each of the knots you have made. The finished splice should have three inconspicuous bumps where you have made the overhand knots.

The Braided Eye Splice

To make an eye splice in ordinary braided line, special tools and techniques are required. The line consists of a hollow braided core enclosed in a braided outer cover; in splicing, these two parts must be separated and a segment of each threaded through the channel of the other. Flexible wire, fashioned into a fid *(opposite)*, is used to open the channels and to draw the lines through.

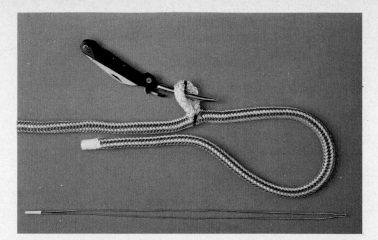

Before beginning the splice, bend a 36-inch length of baling wire into a fid, as shown, securing the ends with tape. Tape the working end of the braided line and tie an overhand knot four feet from the tip; this keeps the line's covering part from slipping down the core. Form a loop the size of the desired eye; pencil a hatch mark on the cover at the point where the splice should begin. Bend the line here, pry apart the cover with a marlinespike and extract a short loop of the core. Make a hatch mark on the core where it emerges from the cover.

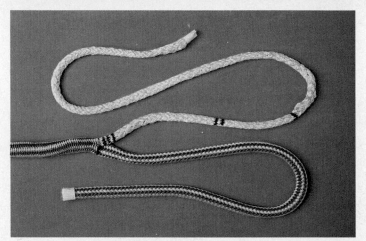

Pull the rest of the core from the working end of the cover. Then continue extracting the core from the standing part—pushing back the cover as you go—until you have pulled out an additional 10 inches. Tape the tip of the core. Two key measurements must now be made on the core. Starting at the hatch mark made on the core, measure off four inches and designate the spot with two pencil marks, as shown. From this double hatch mark, measure six inches to the junction with the cover; identify this spot with three hatch marks.

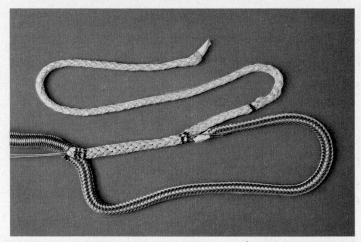

Now comes the actual splicing procedure of running the cover into the core with the fid. Insert the looped end of the fid into the hollow core at the triple hatch mark, thread it through the core and push it out at the double mark. Tightly retape the tip of the cover to give it a point. Slip this tip into the head of the fid so that two to three inches of line are gripped securely between the wires, as shown.

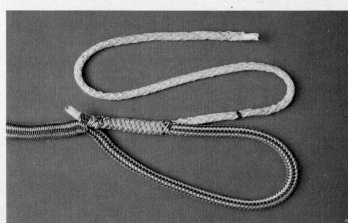

Pull the fid back through the core, drawing the cover with it. This may take considerable effort, since the core's diameter is smaller than the diameter of the cover. But by wiggling the fid back and forth you should be able to force the cover through. Keep pulling until the cover's taped tip emerges at the triple pencil mark. Detach the cover from the fid and work the taped tip back into the core.

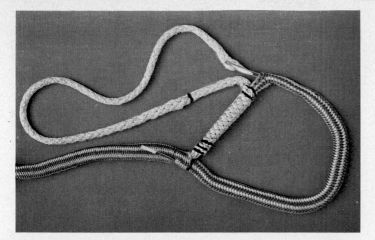

Next, the exposed portion of core will be threaded back into the cover. Begin by inserting the fid into the cover about one half inch below the cover's hatch mark. Make the insertion carefully so the fid does not pick up fibers from the adjacent core. Run the fid through the loop made by the empty cover and bring it out as close as you can to the point where you have just threaded the cover into the core. Now wedge the tip of the core into the head of the fid. Pull on the fid to draw the core back into the cover, as shown.

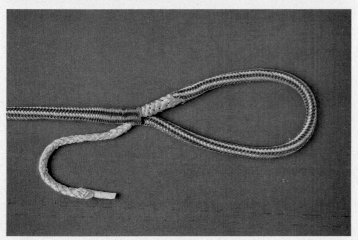

Continue to draw the core through the cover until all the excess has been fed through. Detach the fid and smooth out the loop to ease any bulges. Then start working the bunched portion of the cover —which you pushed back into the standing part in the second step (directly opposite)—forward over the throat of the eye.

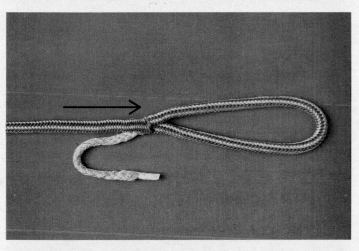

To bring the cover over the bulkiest part of the throat, grab the rope with one hand at the overhand knot you tied in the first step. With the other hand, grip the cover just above the knot and push it up toward the splice (arrow). A sharp, jerking motion is sometimes required to force the cover over the thickest sections of the throat.

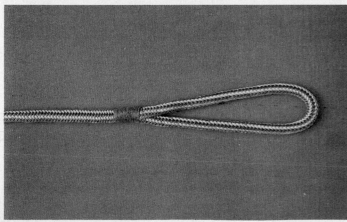

Snip off the tail of the core about one eighth of an inch from the cover. Hold the loop in one hand and the standing part in the other and pull; this pressure on the splice simulates the strain it will be under when in use, and helps to even out the cover. To make sure that the splice will be tight and will not work loose when the line is slack, seize the throat with waxed nylon. The seizing should cover about three inches from the bottom of the loop down the throat.

A Coachwhipped Wheel

For all its trim appearance and sturdy functionality, the shiny metal-rimmed wheel that has become standard equipment on most modern boats of any size has certain practical drawbacks. It can become almost unmanageably slippery when wetted by a rain squall or by wind-blown spray, and in cold weather it is likely to be icy to the touch. However, by wrapping the rim with cotton seine twine —or any similar small-diameter, hard-laid line—the boatman can produce a nonslip surface of relatively constant temperature. Moreover, a neatly wrapped wheel acquires a distinctly salty look, and the wrapping technique is simplicity itself, involving as it does only a single elementary knot—the familiar half hitch.

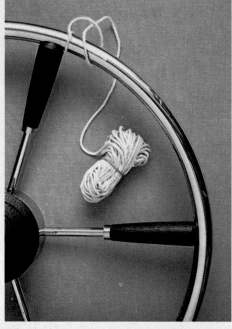

Take the bitter end from a skein of cotton line and lay about six inches along the wheel rim. Starting to the right of a spoke, wind the skein around the rim in a series of half hitches (above), burying the bitter end as you go. Make the hitches in a clockwise direction, passing the working end through each successive turn from right to left.

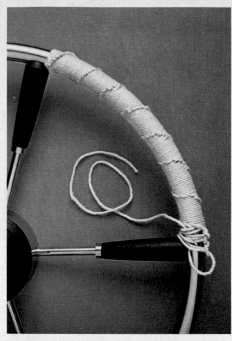

As you finish a segment of rim, make the last few hitches loosely; pass the working end of the line back through these hitches (above), then tighten the hitches and trim off the working end. If all the half hitches have been made alike, the points at which the line passes over itself will fall automatically into a symmetrical spiral pattern, as above.

Continue in the same way to wrap each segment of the rim between one spoke and the next until all segments have been covered. As a final touch, determine which spoke is vertical and uppermost when the boat's rudder is amidships, and tie a Turk's head (pages 116-117) around that spoke to serve as a handy reference for the helmsman.

A Spliced Bridle

A water-ski bridle functions as a strong and flexible link between a skier's towline and the towboat. As explained on page 45, the bridle attaches to a pair of eyebolts, one fixed on either side of the transom. Threaded into the bridle is a lightweight running block, with a shackle for attaching the towline. As the skier slaloms from one side to the other, the running block slides along the bridle so that the drag on each section of line remains equal—so long as neither the skier nor the boat driver turns too abruptly.

While bridles like the one shown here are commercially available in various sizes, a boatman can fashion his own from braided polyethylene water-ski towline, suiting it exactly to his boat's dimensions —and the process will take him no more than 10 minutes' working time.

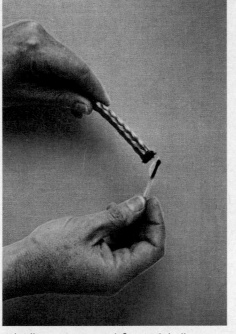

A bridle requires enough 5/16-inch hollow-core polyethylene line to reach from one eyebolt on the towboat's transom to the other, with enough slack to clear the boat's outboard motor or drive unit by about six inches—plus additional line to form two eye splices. Begin the bridle by burning each of the line's two ends with a match (above) until the strands have fused together.

Thread a pair of sister hooks onto one end of the line. Open up a segment of line about 16 inches from the working end by grasping the line about an inch on either side of the selected spot and squashing the line together. At least one opening will appear between the woven braids. Insert the working end into the line's hollow interior (above); push three or four inches of the end back inside the line.

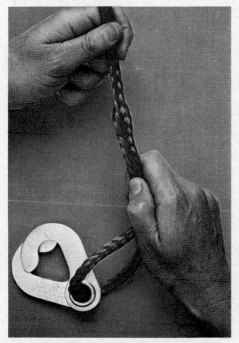

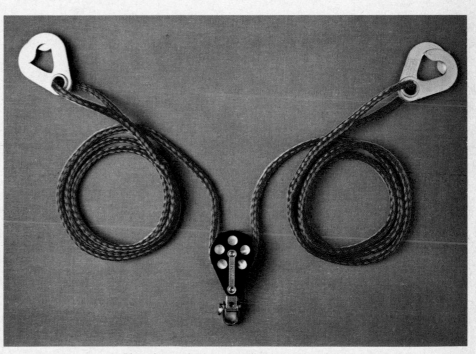

Now grasp the line just above the splice with one hand and below the splice with the other. Pull hard on the splice, as shown above. Since polyethylene line stretches and attenuates slightly under tension, the grip of the strands surrounding the working end will tighten as tension increases. The harder the pull on the splice, the stronger it grows.

Thread onto the line a small lightweight block with a swiveling shackle. Then complete the project by attaching a pair of sister hooks at the other end of the line with an eye splice made the same way as the first. The finished bridle can be clipped securely to the boat by the sister hooks. The water-ski towline attaches to the shackle on the end of the block. To make sure that the weight of the block will not sink the bridle far enough to foul the propeller, fasten a small plastic float onto the towline near its juncture with the block.

A Rope Ladder

A boatman with an hour to spare can contrive a sturdy rope ladder topped off with a chafe-guarded eye for attaching a line. To calculate the amount of manila needed, simply double the desired length of the ladder and add three feet for each rung. The only other material required is a hank of hard-twisted jute for putting a serving of round turns over the eye to bind it securely.

The finished ladder has a variety of uses aboard a boat. It can be slung over the side in a matter of seconds; its round rungs offer firm and comfortable support to a swimmer's bare feet; and it coils neatly away in a deck locker when not in use. A sailor making repeated trips up the mast in the course of a repair job may also find such a ladder a handy alternative to the bosun's chair.

Start the ladder by making the eye. In the middle of the manila line, make a loop three to four inches long. Lay a strand of jute along the left side of the loop and parallel with it, so that the strand's bitter end points toward the top of the loop. Starting near the throat of the loop, bind the rope with jute, covering the bitter end of the jute as you go.

After binding the loop of the eye, continue wrapping jute around the two strands of rope, seizing them together for an inch or so to secure the throat of the eye. Leave a little slack in the last few turns so that you can pass the working end of the jute up under them. Draw these final turns tight around the working end, and cut off any excess jute.

To form the first rung of the ladder, first measure down 10 inches from the throat of the eye. Take the left-hand leg of the ladder and loop it around the right leg. Then pull another loop across to the left. To hold the loops in place, it will help if you lay out the work against a board and drive a nail next to the line, as shown, wherever you change the direction of the lead.

With the working end of the right leg, take enough round turns around the two bights to make a rung five or six inches wide. Work from right to left, and be sure that each turn is snugged up tightly against its neighbors.

When the last turn of the first rung has been completed, pull the working end of the right leg through the loop of the left-hand bight. Note that the right leg has now become the left, and vice versa. Remove the finished rung from the nails and draw the parts up tight. Continue making rungs every 10 inches, taking care to keep the intervals between rungs the same length on both sides.

After finishing the last rung, secure the working ends of the two legs together. The ends can simply be spliced to each other, but a handsomer finale can be achieved, as shown at left, by tying a two-strand Matthew Walker knot and then whipping the ends of the two ropes with marline.

A Knife Lanyard

No sailor should ever be caught without his rigging knife, and a decorative assurance that the knife will always be by his side is a lanyard like the one shown opposite, below. Knotted out of seine twine, it has a loop at one end for threading it into a belt, and a similar loop at the other end for the snap hook that holds the knife. Between the Turk's heads at the throats of the loops are a series of square knots. The work's intricate appearance belies its simplicity—anyone who can tie his shoes can make a lanyard in an afternoon.

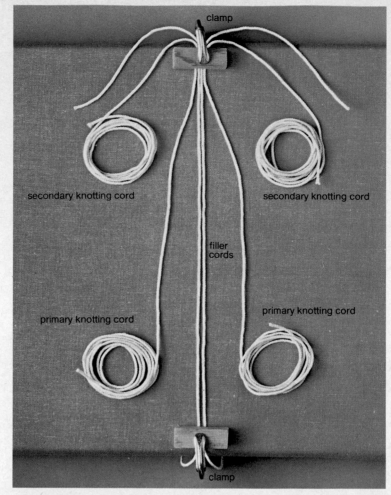

clamp

secondary knotting cord   secondary knotting cord

filler cords

primary knotting cord   primary knotting cord

clamp

To begin making a knife lanyard, clamp side by side, as shown, the bottom ends of two 4-foot lengths of seine twine. These are the filler cords. Clamp the top ends of the filler cords similarly, enclosing in the same clamp and alongside the filler cords the mid-points of two 14-foot lengths of twine. The bottom ends of these two additional lengths of twine are called primary cords; the top ends are the secondary knotting cords. Secure the clamps so the filler cords are stretched taut, as shown at right. You are now ready to start knotting the lanyard.

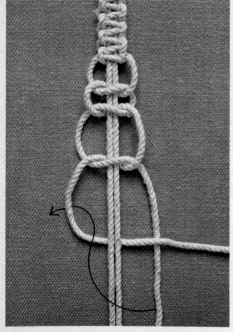

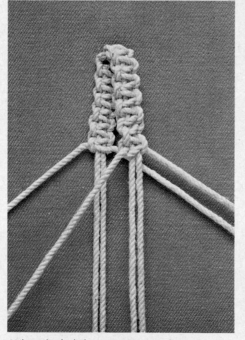

To make the belt loop, tie a series of square knots around the filler cords with the primary knotting cords. Pass the working end of the left-hand knotting cord over the fillers and under the right-hand knotting cord; then pass the right cord under the fillers and through the bight of the left cord. To complete the knot reverse the lead of the knotting cords, as indicated by the arrow.

When the belt-loop section is as long as you want it, unclamp the work. Cut away the filler cords from each end of the knotted strip, sealing the cut ends with dabs of glue. Bring the ends of the strip together to form a loop. Using the two primary knotting cords as a new set of filler cords, tie 10 square knots with the secondary knotting cords.

Now tie 20 half-knots around the new filler cords. Each half-knot is tied, as shown above (arrow), exactly like its predecessor, instead of reversing the lead as in the square knot. The 20 half-knots form a spiral section of lanyard, as shown above and at right. Follow the half-knots with 10 square knots, then 20 more half-knots, then a final section of 10 square knots.

Next, make the section that will form the knife loop. At this point, all four cords become knotting cords. Tie them into a series of four-strand crown knots. This knot is made like the three-strand crown knot (pages 118-119), with each strand passing through a bight of the next strand (above). The resulting chain of knots, designed to resist wear, is known as a four-strand crown sennit.

Thread onto the section of sennit a snap hook for attaching your knife. Form the sennit into a loop, and with two of the four cords used to make the section, tie three or four square knots around the lanyard at the throat of the loop. Trim all four ends and dab with glue.

Tie Turk's head knots (pages 116-117) around the throats of the belt loop and the knife loop, using the same seine twine employed in making the lanyard. To ease the task of making these small Turk's heads, manipulate the twine with a blunt darning needle, as shown above, instead of trying to guide the working end of the twine by hand.

The completed lanyard (left) is a strong and seamanly piece of ropework made interesting by its varied textures. It is long enough to permit free use of the knife but not so long as to be an encumbrance to the wearer.

A Ditty Bag

Every boatman needs a light, stout, stow-able container for the small and easily mislaid articles—marline, shackles, cotter pins, sailmaker's palm and needles, jackknife, beeswax, twine, marlinespike, and the like—that he uses constantly in working around his craft. Since the earliest days of sail, most seamen have stored such gear in a canvas sack called, for reasons now long forgotten, a ditty bag. A sailor usually handcrafted his own bag out of spare swatches of sail canvas and leftover bits of cotton line. Many modern boatmen still make their own ditty bags out of essentially the same materials. By following the pattern and procedures shown here and overleaf, even a novice with the needle can construct a workman-like and long-wearing pouch slung from a strong and handsome lanyard.

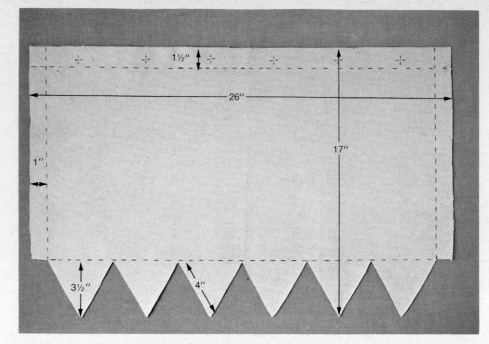

For a handy-sized ditty bag, first cut a rectangle of heavy canvas 17 by 26 inches. Three and one half inches above the bottom edge, draw a line. Starting one inch from one end, notch that side into six equilateral triangles, each four inches on a side and 3½ inches from base to apex, as shown above. These triangles will be sewn together to form the bottom of the bag. Mark a hemline one inch in from each of the two sides and 1½ inches down from the top. Then, ¾ inch down from the top edge, mark positions for six grommet holes, beginning three inches in from one side of the fabric and spacing the centers of the holes four inches apart.

Fold over the top edge along the hemline. Thread a sailmaker's needle with doubled waxed sail twine, and knot the bitter ends together. Then take a series of overcast stitches (Glossary). With the first stitch, bury the knot between the two layers of canvas; subsequent stitches should be about ¼ inch long and ½ inch apart. The bottom of each stitch pierces one thickness of canvas; the top pierces both layers. Finish the hem by running the needle back through a couple of stitches; tie off with a turn around the third stitch. Then use a leather punch or similar tool to make a ⅜-inch diameter hole through both thicknesses of canvas at each of the six grommet marks.

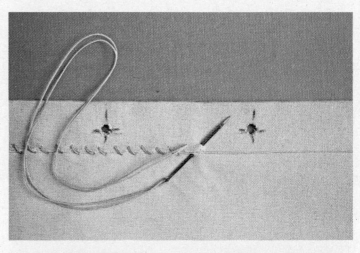

To make a grommet, take several turns of marline around a marlinespike of the intended diameter of the grommet holes. Remove the work from the marlinespike and seize the turns by loosely winding the working end of the marline around them as shown at right (1). Slip the grommet back onto the marlinespike (2) and pull it up hard to draw the seizing tight. Remove the grommet from the marlinespike Trim the ends of the marline, tuck them into the turns and secure them with dabs of glue so the grommet (3) is round and smooth.

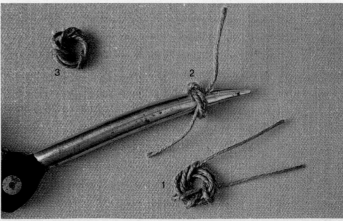

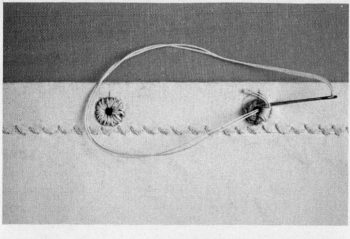

Sew each grommet into its hole, again using doubled sail twine, but this time leaving the bitter end unknotted. Instead, lay ½ inch or so of the bitter end alongside the outer edge of the grommet and bury it as you go. Take each stitch down through the doubled canvas, as shown at left, then up through the hole in the grommet. Keep the stitches close together, overlapping slightly around the inside of the grommet. On completing the circle, run the working end of the twine beneath several stitches, pull it tight and trim it off.

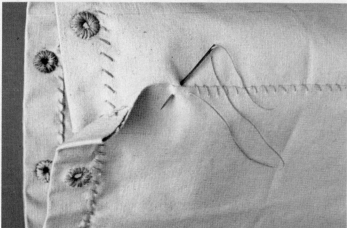

To start the double seam that joins the two sides of the bag, fold over the 1½-inch seam allowance at one end of the canvas. Place this folded edge on top of the seam allowance at the opposite end of the canvas, forming a cylinder. Make sure that the smooth outer face of the seam along the grommeted edge is to the outside of the cylinder. Using a single thread for this first segment of the double seam, sew the doubled edge to the single thickness of canvas beneath it, as shown at left, using the same tools and techniques as for the first seam. The knot securing the bitter end and the knots that finish off the working end should be inside the cylinder.

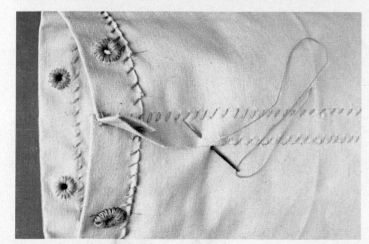

Turn the cylinder inside out so that you are now working on what will be the inside of the completed bag. Where the two edges meet to form the cylinder, you have a single thickness of canvas overlapping a doubled thickness. With a single thread, sew these three thicknesses together as shown at left, using the same overhand stitches as on the other seams. Half of each stitch should pierce one thickness of canvas; the other half pierces three thicknesses. This seam binds the raw edges of canvas to the inside of the bag, finishing the lap seam. Be sure all knots and finishing stitches are inside the bag.

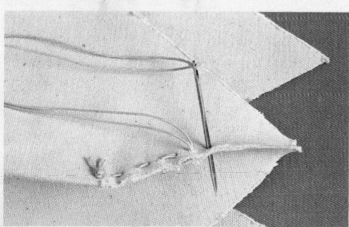

Bring together the adjacent sides of two of the triangles previously cut out along the bottom edge of the canvas. Sew together these sides with a running stitch, as shown at left, about ½ inch in from the edge. As before, keep all knots inside the bag. When all 12 sides of the triangles have been sewed together, take a few more stitches around the center where the apexes of the triangles meet to assure that the finished bag will have a good tight bottom. The bag itself is now complete and awaits only the fashioning of a lanyard (overleaf).

To make the ditty bag's lanyard, seize three 7-foot lengths of ⅜-inch laid-up cotton line at their midpoints with a turn or two of marline. Bend the strands into an eye and serve them with a separate length of ⅜-inch line, as at right. As in forming the eye of the rope ladder (page 130), the bitter end of the serving line is buried under the serving itself; for bulk and symmetry, let the bitter end extend fully around the eye, as here. Remove the temporary marline when convenient. Tuck the working end of the line under the last few turns of the serving, where it extends around the throat of the eye; then draw the serving up tight and trim off the end.

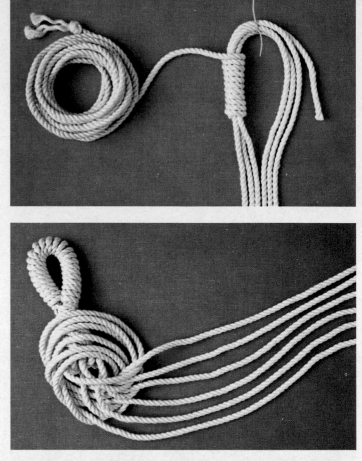

You now have six strands of line depending from the completed eye. Tie the strands into a six-strand Matthew Walker knot (right). The technique is the same as for the three-strand Matthew Walker (pages 120-121) but needs more care to keep the strands in order. Draw the knot up by tightening each strand individually, a little at a time.

Next begin a section of six-strand sennit by tying the strands into a six-strand crown knot made in the same way as the three-strand version (pages 118-119). After completing about five inches of sennit, tie another six-strand Matthew Walker. With a separate length of line, work a Turk's head (pages 116-117) just large enough to fit snugly around the six strands. Thread the strands through the Turk's head.

With the bag turned right side out, begin attaching the lanyard to the grommets. Pass the working end of a strand through a grommet. Unlay about four inches of the working end of the line. Make an ordinary eye splice, tucking each strand back against the lay of the line three times, as you did when making the back splice (page 122). Trim off the ends of the unlaid strands. Similarly attach each remaining line to a grommet. For a particularly neat finish to each splice, you may wish to taper it, progressively trimming off fibers of the unlaid strands as you tuck; then roll the completed splice between your hands, and serve it over with waxed sail twine.

The completed ditty bag (above) is a sturdy and distinctive holdall
that can be hung from any convenient hook—or the boatman's belt if
he is making repairs aloft or up forward on a seaway. The mouth of
the bag can be fully opened up or closed tightly enough to keep
the articles within from falling out simply by sliding the Turk's head
knot up or down the six strands attaching the bag to the lanyard.

5 A trend has developed in recent years to strip down the interiors of pleasure boats, especially sailboats, to the bare essentials, and beyond. The more spartan the accommodations, goes the presumption, the more serious the sailor. And so even some of the slowest, chunkiest family cruising craft are laid out belowdecks with the cold-comfort efficiency of high-performance racing machines, where every ounce of extra weight must earn its way. The stripped-down look means considerable incidental savings both to the owner and the builder, but it is occasionally carried to extremes. Smaller stock cruising craft now come off the line with toilet facilities optional. There is no provision in

GRACE NOTES FOR THE CABIN

admiralty law, however, and indeed there is no nautical tradition that says the cabin of a boat should not be cozy, comfortable and attractive.

Most of the nation's top boating men agree. Yacht designer and master seaman Rod Stephens believes that a boat's living spaces should display all the elegance and distinction of fine antique cabinetry, with "rich, warm wood on the locker fronts, a teak or mahogany dining table, bookshelves, and the evidence of beautiful craftsmanship." Paul Shields, member of a notable racing family from Long Island, went so far as to outfit his power cruiser with a built-in Kleenex box and Velcro pads on the window sills, on which to place Velcro-bottomed vases for flowers.

Such belowdecks grace notes have long been a part of life at sea, not only for cruisers but even aboard racers and working boats. The saloon of the British cutter *Galatea*, which raced for the America's Cup in 1886, had coffered ceilings, Oriental carpets, potted plants, a fireplace and a leopardskin rug. When the portly captain of the whaling ship *Charles W. Morgan* took his slender young wife to sea in 1864, he installed a double bed on gimbals that—to keep in balance—had a box of rocks slung beneath the lady's side as ballast. And many well-equipped Maine fishermen at the turn of the century habitually carried a pot-bellied stove on board with them on winter voyages to take the chill off the cabin air.

Today, almost any cruising craft will benefit from the installation of a small charcoal-burning cabin heater. And any craft, sail or power, looks better with a set of new covers for the bunk cushions. These two projects, along with the others described on the pages that follow, represent a sampling of the ways in which a boatman can add to the livability and attractiveness of his cabin —and they may, in turn, suggest still other projects. The techniques for sewing slip covers, for example, apply equally well to the making of cabin pillows or deck cushions. And the methods for making curtains for the portholes can be used to curtain off entire belowdecks areas—such as the passageway to the forward cabin—for greater privacy. On a fiberglass powerboat, the carpeting for the cabin sole can be extended up the bulkheads to deaden engine noise. And a rack for navigator's tools can, with modifications, be crafted to hold tableware, drinking glasses, binoculars, toothbrushes and a first-aid kit, or virtually any other small gear that the skipper and crew choose to keep aboard for their convenience.

Every boatman will undertake the projects that fit his own tastes, of course. And like mariner-author Carlton Mitchell, whose very personal mahogany-paneled *Finisterre* won the Bermuda race three times running from 1956 to 1960, he may find himself adding embellishments season after season, and to boat after boat. Each of Mitchell's subsequent boats has been increasingly elaborate, and more comfortably appointed belowdecks. "I do not consider I have thrown in the yachting sponge—I have merely widened my scope," Mitchell says. "Home is where the keel is."

A boatman cuts into the cabin overhead, through which he will run the chimney of a charcoal-burning stove—one of many installations that bring cheer belowdecks.

Extra Comfort Below

The belowdecks projects on these pages
—some made with needle and thread,
others with hammer and nails—add to
both the utility and the beauty of a boat.
Carpeting, for instance, helps steady a
passenger's foothold in a choppy sea as
well as visually warming the interior of the
cabin. The carpeting and the other new
projects are colored blue, and described
in detail on the following pages.

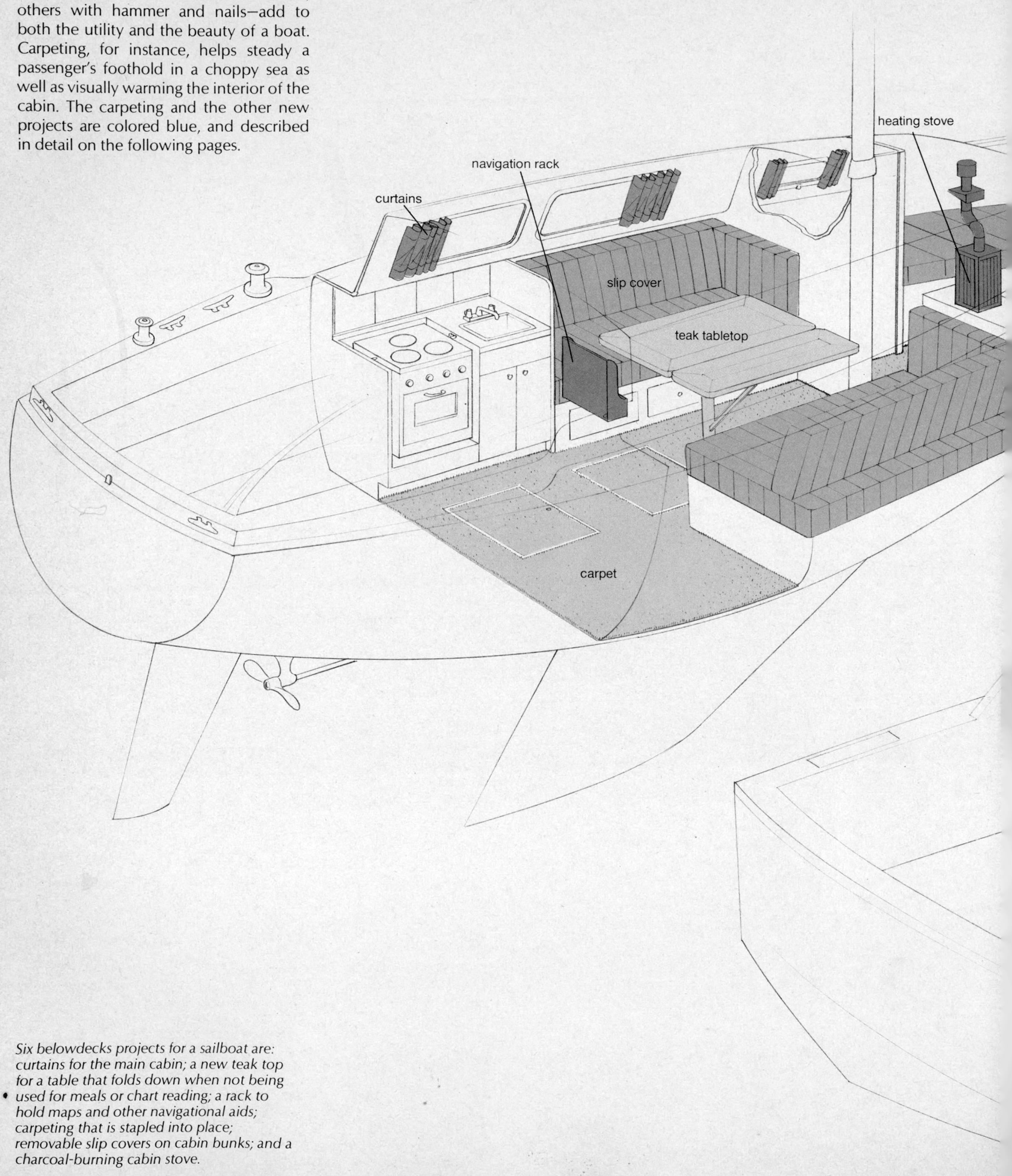

heating stove

navigation rack

curtains

slip cover

teak tabletop

carpet

*Six belowdecks projects for a sailboat are:
curtains for the main cabin; a new teak top
for a table that folds down when not being
used for meals or chart reading; a rack to
hold maps and other navigational aids;
carpeting that is stapled into place;
removable slip covers on cabin bunks; and a
charcoal-burning cabin stove.*

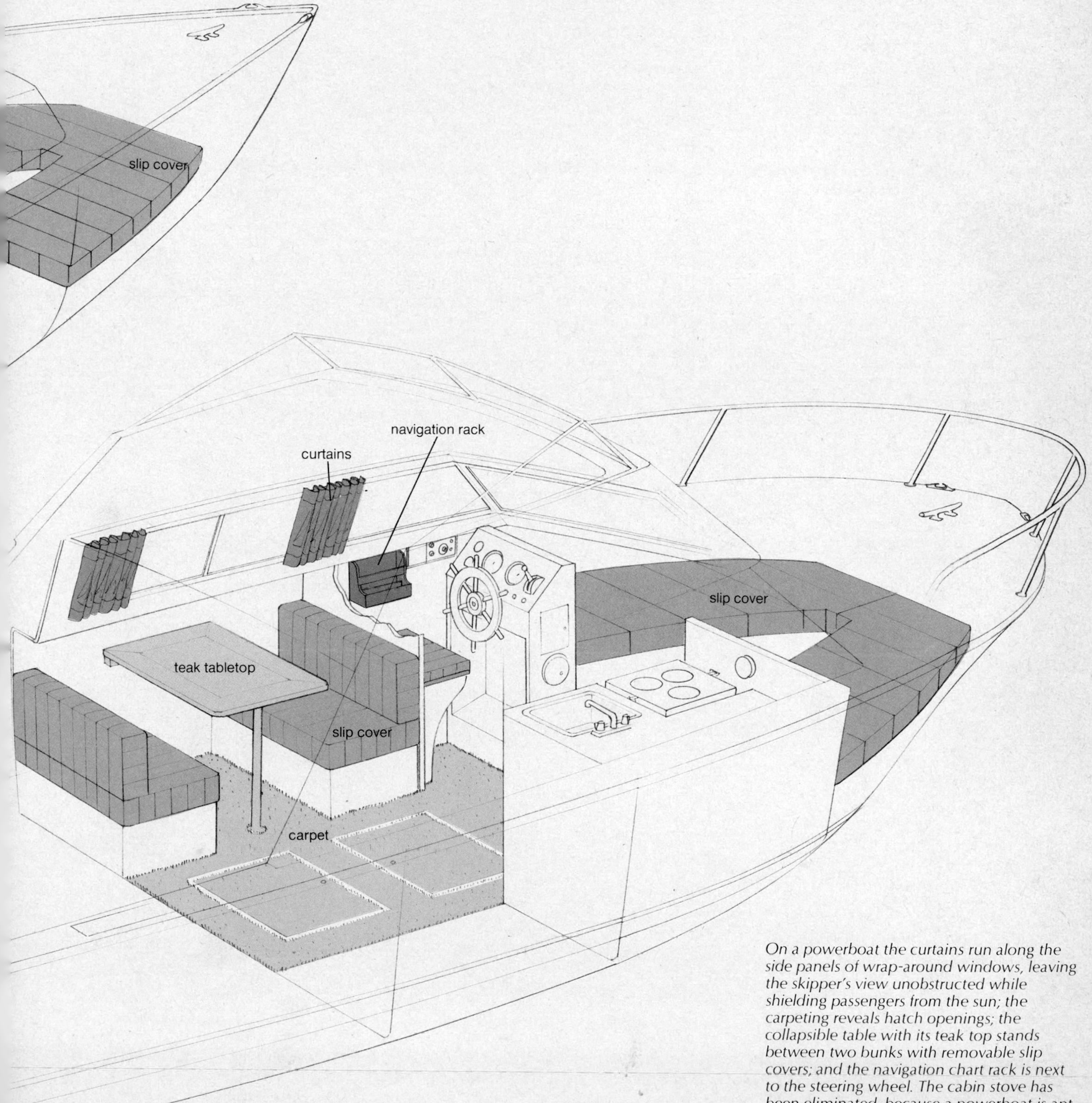

slip cover

curtains

navigation rack

teak tabletop

slip cover

carpet

slip cover

On a powerboat the curtains run along the side panels of wrap-around windows, leaving the skipper's view unobstructed while shielding passengers from the sun; the carpeting reveals hatch openings; the collapsible table with its teak top stands between two bunks with removable slip covers; and the navigation chart rack is next to the steering wheel. The cabin stove has been eliminated, because a powerboat is apt to have a generator, making it possible to warm up any chilly part of the boat with a portable coil heater.

A Rack for the Navigator

Experienced navigators know how important it is to keep basic piloting tools instantly accessible; the partitioned rack shown here is designed to do just that. Its high-backed rear compartment provides room for cruising guides, tide and current tables, light lists and the like; the small guardrail keeps these essential volumés from tipping out. The shallower forward compartment provides a convenient tray for pencils, dividers and parallel rules.

The component parts of the rack can be cut from slightly more than four square feet of any marine-grade ½-inch wood, such as teak or mahogany. Alternatively, wood scraps left over from some other project may well serve for this trimly proportioned fixture. If none of the individual scraps are wide enough to make up the rack's back piece, two widths can be fitted together, as in the example shown.

The carpentry procedures required are simple even for a beginner; in fact, the entire project can be completed using manual tools to substitute for the electric ones commonly employed: a saber saw, an electric drill and a belt sander. The finished rack is then fastened through its back to the bulkhead by means of a screw set into each corner.

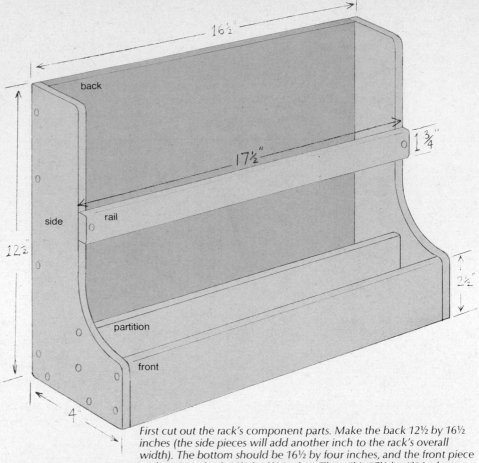

First cut out the rack's component parts. Make the back 12½ by 16½ inches (the side pieces will add another inch to the rack's overall width). The bottom should be 16½ by four inches, and the front piece and partition both 16½ by 2½ inches. The rail is 17½ by 1¾ inches.

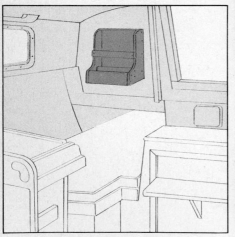

One of the most convenient places to install a navigator's rack is on the cabin bulkhead next to the companionway, where it is quickly accessible from topside and also close to the belowdecks chart table.

To cut out the curved front edge of the side pieces, first inscribe two parallel lines on a 12½-inch teak scrap as follows: indent the first line two inches, in order to mark the narrow upper section of the side piece. Indent the second line 5¼ inches, marking the short, wider section that joins the shelf front. Mark a point 2½ inches from one end of this second line. Using a pencil compass, draw an arc that passes through this point and just touches the first line. Cut along the completed outline with a saber saw and repeat the process on a similar 12½-inch piece of wood to form the second side.

Begin the assembly by joining the side pieces to the back. Draw guidelines, indented ¼ inch, on a side piece along the 12½- and five-inch edges to position the screws. Place the back in a vise—section by section, if necessary, as here—and fit the side piece to it. Drill screw holes with a countersink bit, and set the screws. Fasten the remaining back, side and bottom pieces similarly.

Next, make a guideline for screwing in the shelf partition. On the exterior surface of each side piece, draw a vertical line 2¾ inches from the back edge of the rack. Have a helper hold the partition in place, as shown, so that its rear surface is exactly two inches from the back piece. The partition should now be centered along the guideline. Drill holes and fit two screws into the partition through the guideline. In the same manner, fit and screw down the front piece, making the guideline 4¾ inches from the back edge of the rack.

Lay the rack on its back and attach the front guardrail, positioning its upper edge five inches down from the top of the rack. Fill all screw holes with bungs, using the methods described on page 29. Finally, sand the exterior of the rack, smoothing the bungs, rounding any sharp edges and erasing all pencil marks on the wood. Oil the rack with teak oil and fasten it to the bulkhead with screws.

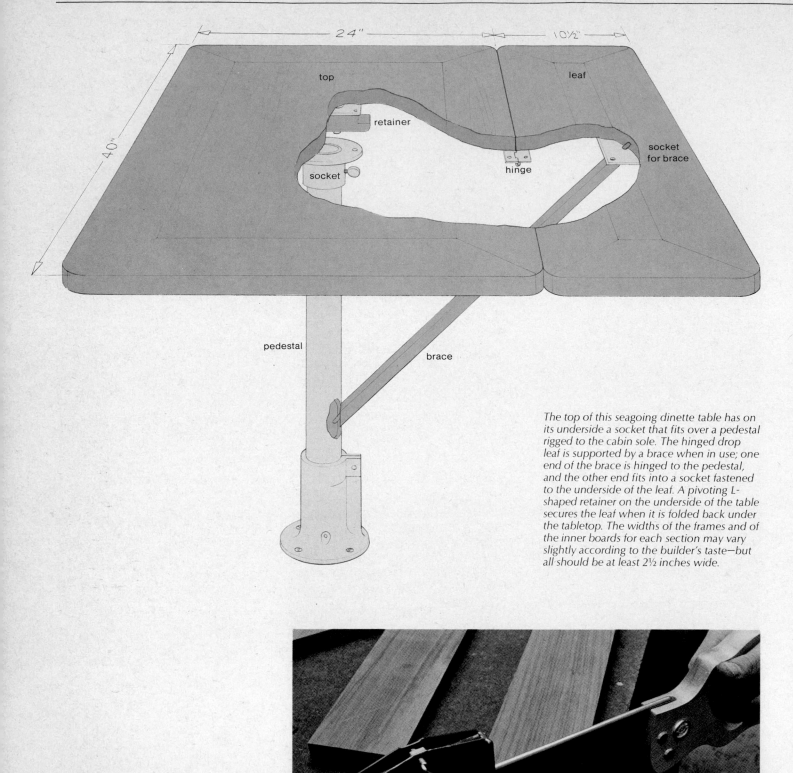

24"

10½"

top

leaf

retainer

socket for brace

40"

socket

hinge

pedestal

brace

The top of this seagoing dinette table has on its underside a socket that fits over a pedestal rigged to the cabin sole. The hinged drop leaf is supported by a brace when in use; one end of the brace is hinged to the pedestal, and the other end fits into a socket fastened to the underside of the leaf. A pivoting L-shaped retainer on the underside of the table secures the leaf when it is folded back under the tabletop. The widths of the frames and of the inner boards for each section may vary slightly according to the builder's taste—but all should be at least 2½ inches wide.

In cutting the boards to their proper size, use a table saw with a sharp blade to ensure that all edges are smooth and square. Miter three of the four frame pieces—the two sides and one end—using a backsaw and a miter box (right) or a circular saw.

Teak for a Table

Many stock-built cruising boats today come with a pedestal-mounted dinette table already installed. But these tables generally have Formica tops, which not only have a tendency to scar, but look too much like a home kitchen accessory to suit the tastes of many sailors. The answer is to replace the Formica with a handsome, functional top of teak boards arranged in an attractive pattern.

To make a tabletop, the boatman first must calculate the overall dimension of both the main top section and the leaf that will hinge to it. Then he should purchase enough ⅞-inch-thick teak boards to cover the total area—plus a 15 per cent spoilage allowance. With this lumber on hand, he constructs first the leaf, as shown here and on the following pages, then, by employing the same methods, assembles the top.

In each case, he cuts the boards to the desired sizes and fastens them together with dowels and resorcinol glue. To install the dowels he needs a doweling jig, which will allow him to drill dowel holes that are straight, centered—and positioned so that the dowels inserted into one board will fit precisely into holes drilled in an adjoining board. The best dowels to use are commercially available ⅜-inch-diameter dowels that come already cut to two inches in length, with beveled ends for easy entry and spiral grooves to help spread glue inside the holes.

As a final step, the boatman sands and finishes the top and its leaf, attaches the hardware shown in the drawing at left, and installs the new top into his boat.

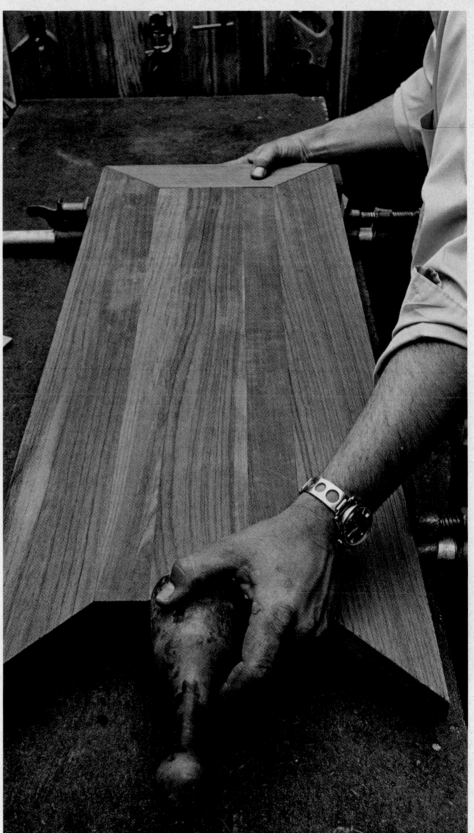

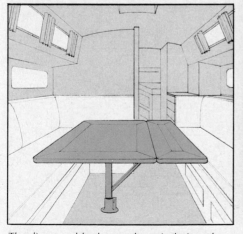

The dinette table shown above is designed so that, with the hinged leaf extended, it offers an ample surface well within reach of people seated along the sides of the cabin. Folding the leaf down and under the tabletop creates a passageway for traffic through the cabin, or provides room for making up a bunk on that side of the table.

With the boards cut, lay the inside pieces—flanked by the two sides of the frame—across two pipe clamps. Lightly clamp the assembly together. Hold the end piece of the frame against one end of the assembly. With a mallet, jog the other ends of the inside pieces into precise alignment (above). Tighten the clamps. Miter another end piece to fit the space left for it. Number each piece for easy reassembly. Mark positions for dowels (overleaf) with straight lines drawn across the assembly at six-inch intervals, starting 1½ inches in from the ends of the inside pieces.

To begin doweling, put a ⅜-inch bit through the guide until its tip rests on the board. Mark the bit with tape 1 inch above the top of the guide. Drill until the tape touches the guide. Hold the tool steady, and do not force the bit against the marking tape. Repeat the drilling, leaving a series of 1-inch-deep holes along the inside edges of the two side frames and both edges of each inside piece.

Dip 2-inch dowels in glue and insert them into the holes in a side frame. Spread glue along the edges of the frame and the adjacent inside piece (below). Tap the two boards together, fitting the dowels in the frame into the corresponding holes in the inside piece. Similarly join the remaining inside boards and the other side frame. Then clamp the completed assembly and let it dry overnight.

Set the two end frames in place, making sure that they still fit snugly. Starting 1½ inches in from the inner corners of the frame, draw dowel lines across the end frames and onto the inside pieces. As you did before, drill holes, insert dowels, spread glue on all joining surfaces, and tap the end frames into place with a mallet (above), protecting their outside edges with a scrap of wood.

Clamp the assembly tightly lengthwise with pipe clamps. The longitudinal pressure will force the outer corners of the end frames up and out of alignment with the side frames. Sandwich each corner between two flat scraps of wood and compress each of the corners back into alignment with a C clamp. Let the now completely assembled leaf dry overnight.

Remove all clamps. Sand both surfaces of the completed leaf with a belt sander, using first medium and then fine sandpaper. Finish by hand-sanding at the corners where the grains of adjacent boards run in different directions. Scribe a curve of whatever size pleases your eye at each corner; cut around the curves with a saber saw (above) and hand-sand the rounded corners.

After finishing the leaf and a similarly constructed tabletop, attach the socket to the center of the table's underside. Attach the leaf to the top with 3 marine brass butt hinges. Put the table in place on the pedestal. Prop the leaf up horizontally. Determine and mark the proper location of the socket for the brace. Remove the top and its attached leaf from the pedestal and install the brace socket. Finally, attach to the underside of the tabletop the metal fitting for the pivoting teak retainer (above), which will hold the leaf in place when it is folded back under the tabletop.

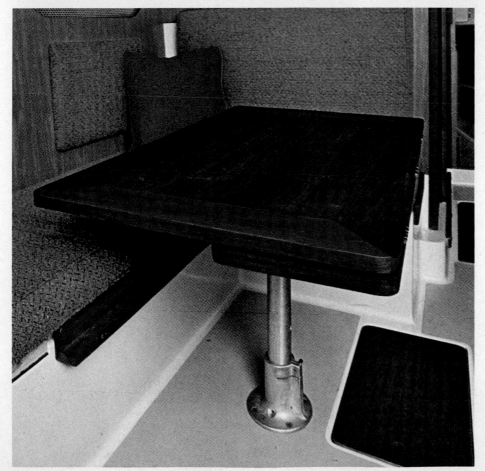

The completed tabletop installed on its pedestal adds a sumptuous air to the cabin. Depending on the tastes of the owner, the upper surface of a teak top like this one can be washed down with an acetone solution and then brushed with polyurethane, or given a natural finish by rubbing with teak oil.

Covers for Cushions

After a few seasons' use at sea, the cloth covers of cabin bunk cushions will almost certainly begin to show signs of wear. Replacing them with new covers extends the life of the cushions and brightens up the cabin to boot. Any boatowner who has a passing acquaintance with fundamental sewing techniques and access to a sewing machine can create new slip covers—provided that a few of the special precautions demanded by seagoing sewing projects are observed.

Materials should be chosen with an eye to withstanding a hard climate and usage. Thread must be a nonrotting synthetic variety. The sturdiest soft-surfaced cloth is made from nonabsorbent synthetic fibers called olefins, which are bonded to a stiff latex backing. Sailcloth, whipcord, canvas and gabardine are also good fabrics for marine use; they can be bought pretreated for mildew resistance, and most professional cleaners can treat them for fire retardancy. Marine vinyl is another good choice, especially for the undersides of interior cushions—as well as for all those that are to be used above decks. It is mildewproof, extremely resistant to sun, soil and most chemicals, and doesn't shrink or stretch.

In ordering the other necessary materials, be sure to get noncorroding plastic zippers that are four inches shorter than the length of the cushion's back. Each cushion also requires shrinkproof cord for welting, which is the tubular trim that runs along the cushion's top and bottom pieces and closes the seams. And the boatowner should also have on hand brown paper for the pattern, a metal ruler, a pencil, some chalk and pins.

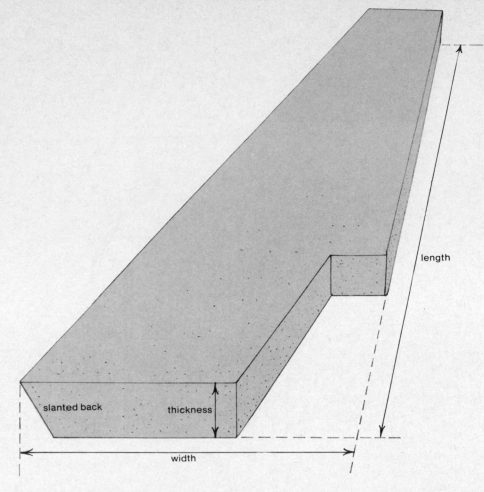

To determine the amount of fabric for each of the two V-berth cushions, double the cushion's overall length to obtain the yardage for the top and bottom pieces, then add another yard for every 20 yards of welting. To calculate the length of welting, measure the perimeter of the cushion top, double this figure and add 25 inches. There will be enough fabric for the side pieces, called boxing, in the leftover pieces from the bolt of cloth cut for the top, the bottom and the welting. Note that since the cushion back is slanted, the width of the top and bottom pieces will have to be calculated separately when making up the pattern pieces (below).

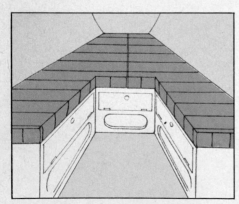

New covers for the irregularly contoured, matching pair of V berths shown here require perhaps the most careful measuring and sewing of any mattress or cushion aboard ship. Yet they should take even a casual craftsman roughly four hours per cover.

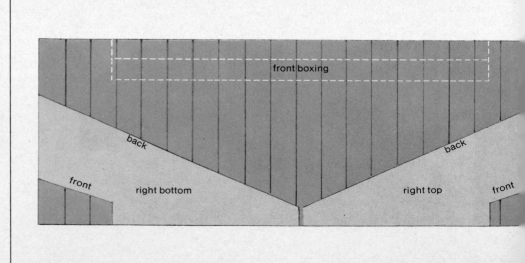

To make the patterns for the cushions, begin by placing one cushion, top down, on a double layer of brown paper. Insert a metal ruler underneath the cushion edge (left) to guide your pencil, and trace all around the cushion, moving the ruler as necessary. Remove the cushion; cut along the line through both pieces of paper. Turn the cushion bottom side down on another double layer of paper and repeat. Label each piece. There is no need to make boxing patterns; they will be drawn directly on the cloth.

Place the fabric right side up. Pin on the pattern pieces, aligning their front edges with the selvage—the finished edge of the weave. Match up any designs on the fabric. Outline the boxing strips as follows: use one strip for the front and sides of each cushion, adding an inch at each end and an extra inch of width for seam allowance. Draw two strips, with the same seam allowance and length, for each cushion back; make each strip half the cushion thickness (the zippers will be sewn between two halves). Cut and label all pieces. Then draw and cut ¾-inch-wide diagonal—or bias—strips for the welting.

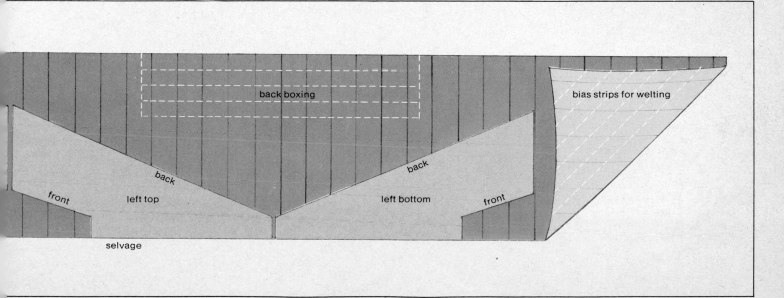

Begin the sewing stage of the project by fashioning the welting. Turn each bias-cut strip wrong side up; across both ends, mark a chalk line ⅜ inch from the edge for seam allowance. Join two strips at right angles (inset), with their right sides facing each other. Stitch along the chalk mark. Join the remaining bias pieces in the same fashion to form one long welting strip. Fold the strip, right side out, around welting cord; then align the edges, and run a line of machine stitches close to the cord, as shown.

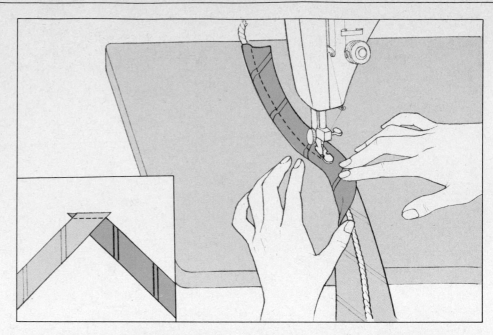

To install the zipper, place two back boxing strips atop one another, wrong sides out, and stitch down one side, ½ inch from the edge. Open the fabric wrong side up and flatten the seam allowances. Center the closed zipper, face down, along the seam and pin it in place. At the top of the zipper tape, stitch down one side and around the tape's circumference. Turn the boxing strip right side up; remove the stitches covering the zipper.

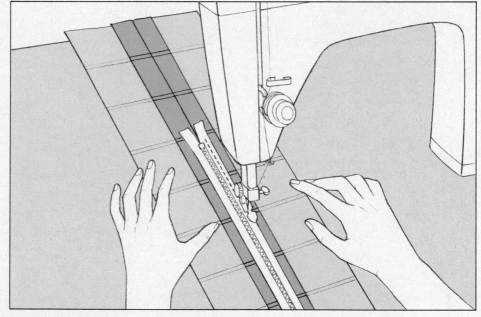

Now attach the welting to the cushion tops and bottoms. Place the fabric right side up, align its edges with the welting, and pin, as shown. Stitch close to the cord. When nearing an inside corner, stop the machine, pinch the cord into the corner, pin and resume stitching. Near an outside corner, stop and snip a small cut in the welting seam allowance; pin the welting in place and resume stitching. After stitching the welting around the cushion top's perimeter, sew the welting ends together.

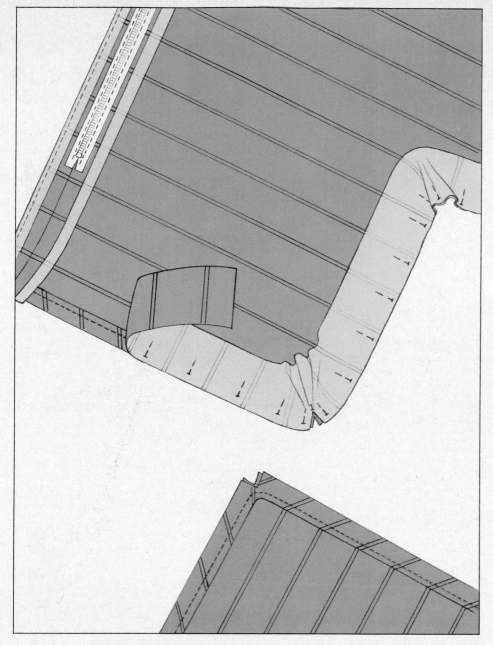

Lay the cushion top right side up and pin on the front boxing strip; make sure that all the seam allowances run along the outside, as shown. As in the preceding step, slit the seam allowance for outside corners, and pinch inside corners. Stitch to within two inches of the ends of the boxing. Then align the back boxing with the back of the cushion top, pin, and stitch the full length of the cushion—but leave the ends unsewed. Stitch the corners, allowing for the taper of the cushion, then finish attaching the boxing. Open the zipper five inches; sew the cushion's bottom piece to the boxing's lower edge.

Now turn the finished cushion cover right side out and slip it onto its proper V-berth mattress. The cover should fit as tightly and smoothly as a skin. The zipper running along the back boxing will be concealed when the cushion is placed on the berth.

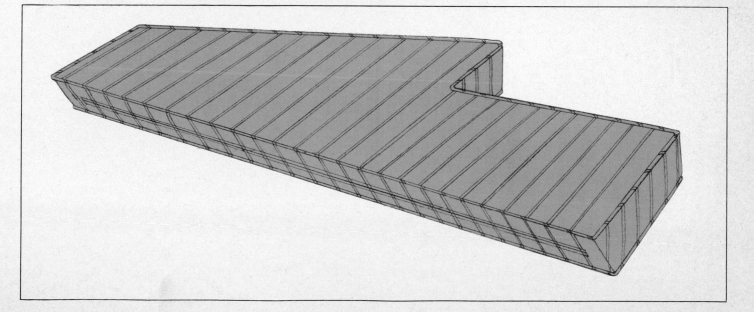

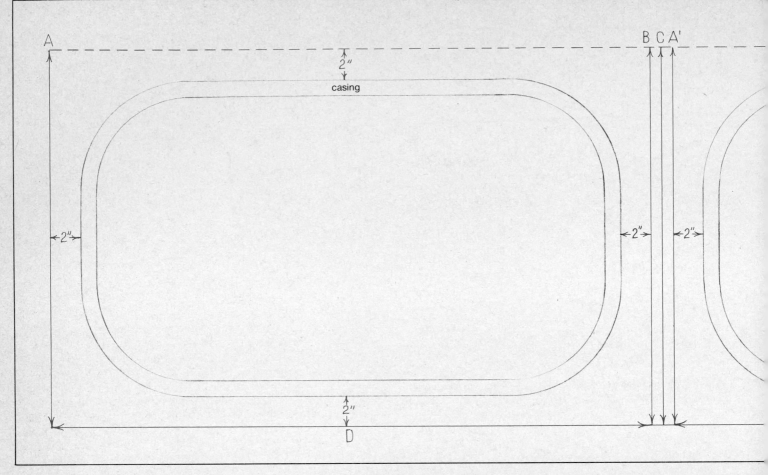

Mark guidelines for setting the curtains' track or tracks 2 inches above porthole casings and extending 2 inches beyond each casing. This line will act as a base measurement for determining fabric needs, as follows: for a single porthole measure the track line (A to B) and double this width to account for pleats. For curtains over 2 adjoining ports, as here, measure from point A to the center point between the ports (C) and double. For length, measure from the track line to 2 inches below (D) the casing. Add 8 inches for hems. For lining, add 4 inches for hems, on single-track curtains, none for double. For tape length, double the track line of the curtains and add 8 inches.

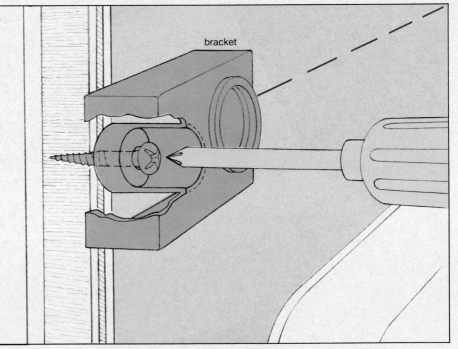

Begin the track installation by positioning an end bracket at one end of the track line, and marking the screw hole. Remove the bracket, drill a hole—no deeper than half the thickness of your bulkhead material—replace the bracket and screw into place.

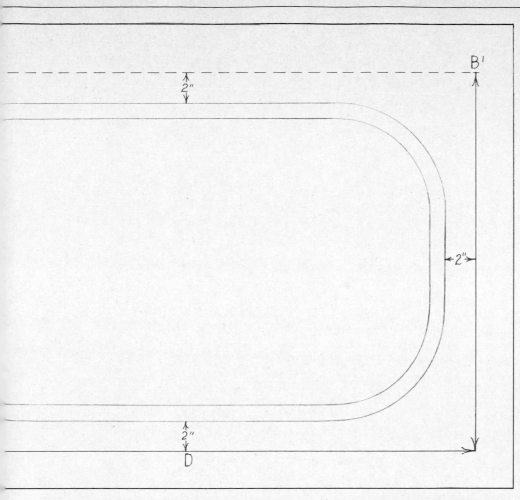

B'

2"

2"

2"

D

Curtains for Ports

Putting curtains on a boat's porthole makes the craft more livable in a number of ways. Besides looking pretty and affording privacy at dockside, they can act as insulators, screening out direct sunlight on hot days and keeping in a measure of cabin warmth on cold ones. They also help absorb sound. For the best sound and temperature control—and to prevent the fabric colors from fading in the sun—curtains should be lined. The addition of pleats to the basic design helps the curtains hang more evenly.

Choose fabric that has been treated to be colorfast and mildew resistant. For lining, use white insulated curtain lining. If pretreated fabric is not available, choose good quality cotton blended with a synthetic such as polyester for the curtains, and for the lining use white cotton. Then spray your finished curtains with waterproofing fabric spray.

The best mounting for the curtains is a plastic track like the one shown here. Such tracks, which come in three-foot sections, are flexible enough to follow curving bulkheads, and can be cut to any length. They have predrilled screw holes and end brackets so that installation is simple. On the track are sliding plastic carriers with snap holes. The other halves of the snaps are on a specially made fabric tape that is sewn to the top of the curtains and then snapped onto the carriers. For covering portholes on slanted bulkheads or for added safety in the galley, use a double set of tracks to hold the curtains securely top and bottom.

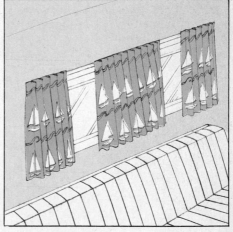

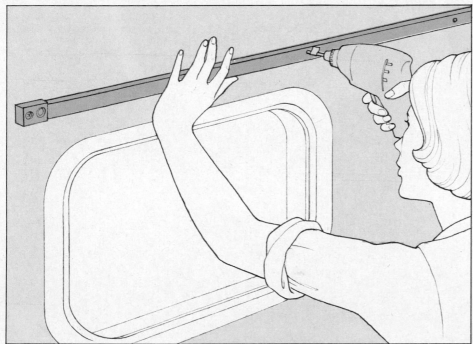

Slip the end of the track into the end bracket; position the track along the guideline and mark each screw hole for drilling. If the track must be cut off, mark the cut line at this time, making the track itself one half inch less than the guideline to leave space for the other end bracket. With a hack saw, cut the track. Reinsert it into the first end bracket, screw it into place, slip on the second end bracket and mark the hole. Drill the hole and install the second bracket. Repeat the procedure when adding a second or a bottom track.

Cabin curtains can be hung separately, with an individual track over each porthole. Or, where two or more portholes of the same dimension lie side by side, as in the picture above, the curtain sets can be hung on one continuous piece of track. In either instance, the curtains are made in separate panels, which can be adjusted independently.

Cut the required number of fabric sections and lay them on a work surface wrong side up. If two pieces of fabric are needed to make up a panel and one is narrower, as at right, machine stitch them together so the narrower piece will hang on the side of the porthole. Clip across any selvage (finished edges of the fabric) at intervals to keep the seams from puckering. Fold the bottom of each curtain up two inches to make a partial hem; press, then fold over two inches again and press. Fold and press the top hem in the same manner. Machine stitch the bottom hem if the curtain is to have a single track.

Cut lining panels that will be five inches shorter and four inches narrower than their corresponding unhemmed curtain panels. Fold a double two-inch hem at the lining bottom and machine stitch it. Lay the right sides of curtain and lining panels together with the lining hem an inch above the bottom hem of the curtain. Stitch the sides together from top to bottom with one-inch seams and turn the lined curtain right sides out. Fold the top double two-inch curtain hem down over the lining top and pin. Then hand baste this hem to the lining. Tack the side hems to the bottom at the lower corners.

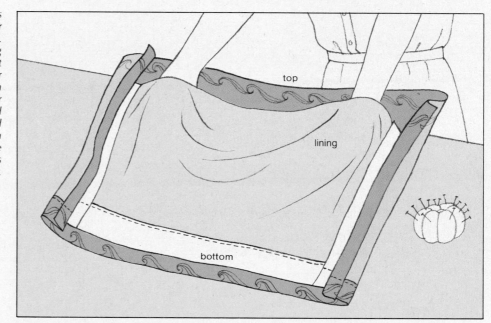

Center a length of snap tape along the inside top hem of the panel so that a snap falls as near as possible to one inch from each end. If necessary, take a little tuck in the tape at each end to bring the end snaps into position. Trim the tape ½ inch beyond each edge of the panel, then pin it so the top edge aligns with that of the curtain and the extra ½ inch at each end is folded under itself. Stitch completely around the tape, starting at the top edge. For double-track curtains, repeat all tape steps on the bottom hem.

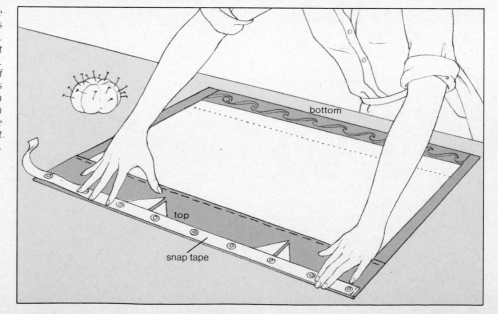

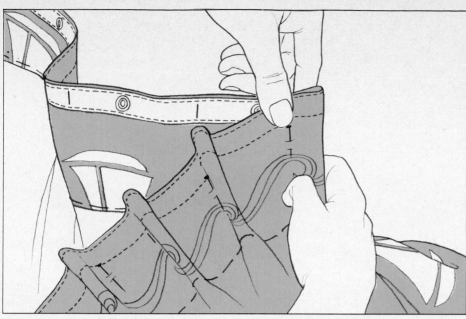

To make pleats, first mark and count the center points between snaps. Then measure the width of the hemmed panel. To calculate how deep each pleat should be, divide the track-line measurement in half and subtract this amount from the panel width. Divide by the number of spaces between snaps. Halve that result to get the depth of the pleat. Fold the panel at each marking between snaps, measure to the correct depth and pin. Stitch each pleat along the pin line for the full width of the hem. Remove the basting in the top hem and tack the hem to the lining.

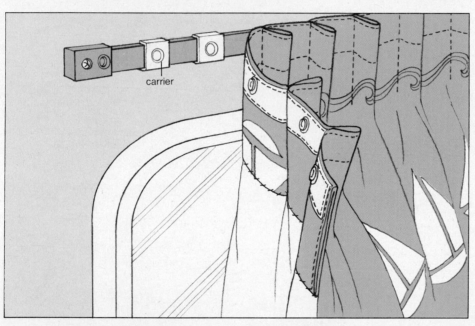

carrier

To hang the finished curtains, first put sufficient plastic snap carriers onto the track. Then begin attaching the curtain at one of the end brackets and work toward the other end. Remember that a final snap should attach to each end bracket. Repeat with bottom snaps on a double track.

An Alternate Fixture

This alternate type of marine curtain rod uses tabs inserted in a channel track rather than snaps to attach the curtain. The tab system is cheaper, has fewer pieces, and the track can be bought cut to size. However, the curtains will hang from the track a little more loosely than they do with the snap tape, and an end plug must be unscrewed and removed from one end of the track to take the curtains down. The curtains are made the same as for snap tapes—with one exception: the tab tape is attached one inch below the top edge, and for double track, one inch above the bottom so that the finished curtains will cover the track. To allow for this adjustment, add nine inches of fabric instead of eight for single-track hems and 10 inches for double.

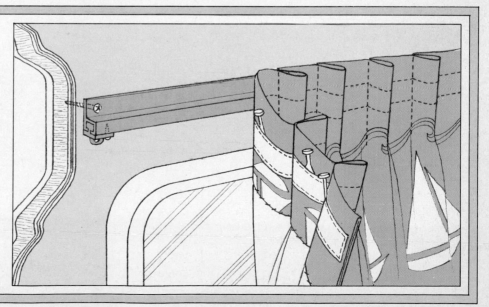

Carpets for the Cabin

Carpeting, once rarely found in pleasure craft, now is used in most powerboats —and in many sailboats—to enhance the appearance of a cabin, protect plywood cabin soles, provide comfortable nonskid footing and muffle engine noise. To install carpeting, the boatman first determines the full dimensions of his cabin sole with a tape measure, then buys enough carpet to cover the sole with a few inches to spare on all sides. He should select a carpet with pile and backing of a durable, waterproof synthetic—nylon, acrylon or polypropylene. These fabrics will resist stains, mildew and rot better than natural fibers and will not ravel when cut.

The only minor problem in laying the carpet is that it must not block hatches that give access to engines and other vital areas. One way to be sure such hatches remain accessible is to slit the carpet so that a flap can be pulled back, enabling the boatman to get at the covers *(page 159)*. A more traditional method is to carpet each hatch cover individually, using a template as a guide in cutting the hatch-cover pieces. When an existing floor covering is being replaced, the old carpet serves as the template. For a first-time installation, the boatman makes a paper template for each segment of sole he intends to cover.

In either case, he spreads out the new carpet *(right, below)*, lays his templates over it and cuts out the various pieces. After carpeting each hatch cover, he installs the rest of the carpet, using a carpet-stretcher *(page 159)*, a device available in many tool-renting establishments.

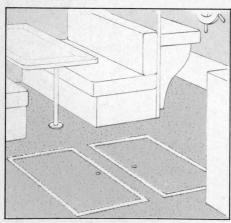

The saloon of this powerboat shows how a vessel's interior can be enhanced by carpeting. A single piece of carpet has been cut to fit around the hatch covers—which have been individually carpeted—and around irregularities in the cabin sole's outline, such as the steering console. Other areas that can be carpeted include fore and aft cabins, cockpits, bulkheads and cabin overheads.

Begin by measuring the cabin sole and make sure when buying new carpet that your measurements include the sole's greatest dimensions —with a little excess for safety. Remove the old carpet, starting with the separate pieces attached to the hatch covers. An easy way to begin is to stick an awl through a corner of the carpeting, pry up the corner *(below)* and pull. Remove all tacks or staples that remain in the wood after the carpet has been taken up. If the carpet has been glued down, you may have to scrape a residue of cement and bits of carpet backing from the surface of the hatch cover.

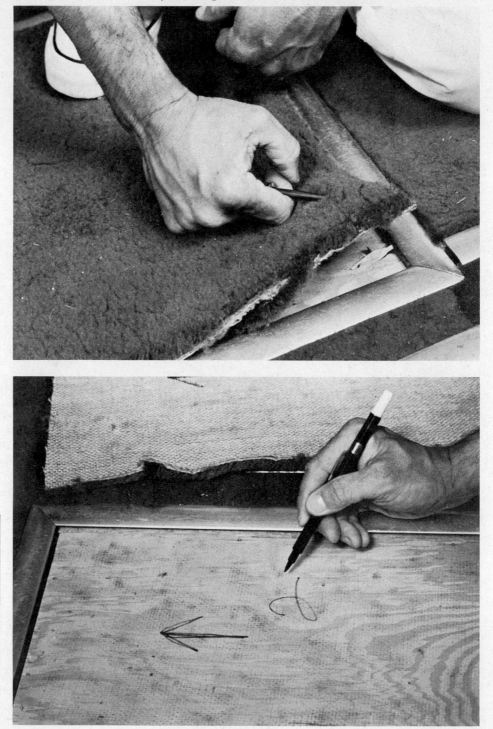

As you remove each hatch-cover piece, mark an identifying number on its reverse side and on the hatch cover beneath. Mark on each an arrow *(above)* indicating which way the grain of the new carpet will run. The grain is the direction in which the fibers of pile naturally incline; to avoid a patchy effect, the separate pieces of carpeting should be laid with their grains running in the same direction.

Spread out the new carpet face down on a dock or other ample, flat area. Lay on top of it, face down and in their proper order, the paper templates or the pieces of old carpet being used as templates. If in doubt about the positions of the pieces in this giant jigsaw puzzle, refer to the identifying numbers marked on the cabin sole. Mark around the edges of each hatch-cover template and cut along the marks with a carpet knife (left). Always cut down through the backing when cutting or trimming carpet to avoid shearing off pile along the cut.

As each hatch-cover piece is cut from the new carpet, lay aside the corresponding template of old carpeting (above) to avoid confusing it with other templates. Copy on the back of each new hatch-cover piece the identifying number and grain-direction arrow from the back of the template. When all hatch-cover pieces have been cut out, match each one with its proper hatch cover and begin installing (overleaf).

Align a hatch-cover piece on its corresponding hatch cover. Trim off any excess carpet. If the cover has flat metal moldings attached with screws to the upper surface of the cover, remove screws and moldings. Realign the carpet on the cover and reattach the moldings, sandwiching the edges of the carpet between the hatch cover and the moldings. Moldings that are T-shaped in cross section and attached to the edges of a hatch cover need not be removed. Simply use a short, stiff putty knife or similar tool to tuck the edges of the carpet under the lip of the molding (below).

To make room in the carpet for the shaft of a bolt-type hatch lifter, cut a small slit in the edge of the carpet above the lifter and snug the slit down around the lifter (below). To provide access to a ring-type lifter, mark and cut a small circle in the carpet above the lifter.

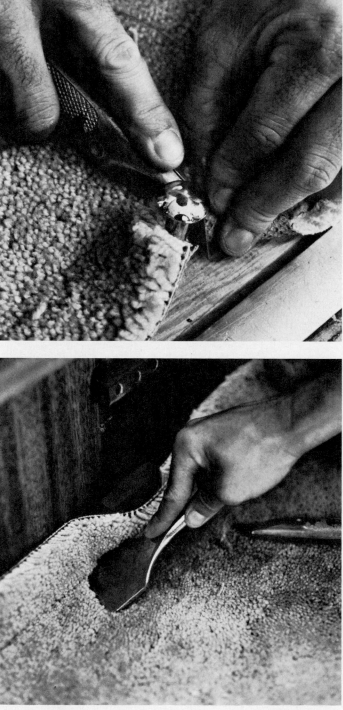

A quick, secure and easy way to attach the carpet to the hatch cover is to staple it along all four edges at intervals of two or three inches. A hand-operated staple gun will drive a 9/16-inch stainless-steel staple through most carpet backings and into the plywood cabin sole below. For a smooth, invisible stapling job, part the fibers of the pile as you staple (above), so that the staples do not catch any of the pile. When properly done, the pile closes over and conceals the staples. After carpeting all hatch covers, spread the remainder of the carpet over the rest of the cabin sole.

Adjust the remaining carpet to fit around the newly carpeted hatch covers and staple it carefully around the covers, with the staples an inch or so from each edge. To mark for trimming any excess at the outer edges along the bulkheads, run the corner of a broad, blunt chisel along the carpet's face at the juncture of the cabin sole and each bulkhead (above) in turn. Press hard enough to make a slight ridge on the backside of the carpet. Trim along this ridge.

To prevent wrinkles, stretch the carpet both fore and aft and amidships during installation. Align one long edge of the carpet along the edge of the cabin sole and staple it. Use a carpet stretcher to align the opposite edge, a few feet at a time. Set the adjustable spikes in the head of the stretcher so they are long enough to grip without piercing the carpet. Place the stretcher, spikes down, near the edge of the carpet (above). Nudge the stretcher's padded end sharply with your knee, pushing the carpet to the sole's edge. Trim if necessary, stretch the carpet edge to the sole's edge again and staple.

Similarly attach the two remaining edges of the main carpet, first stapling down one edge, then stretching the fabric with the carpet stretcher and finally stapling down the remaining edge. The completely carpeted sole (below) combines nautical neatness with an aura of elegance—while still allowing instant access to hatches.

Careful Concealment

Nowadays the cabins of ever-increasing numbers of boats are being covered with what appears to be unbroken, wall-to-wall carpeting. This living-room look, however, can be somewhat deceiving. Usually, this type of carpet has been slit in such a way that a segment of it can be peeled back to provide access to hatch covers that lie concealed beneath.

The carpet shown at right has been slit along three sides of a rectangle and stapled down along the outer edges of the slits. Along the inner edges of the slits, strips of Velcro tape have been glued to the underside of the carpet and to the sole immediately underneath. When the strips are pressed together, the Velcro holds the carpet in place and the pile of the carpet conceals the slits. Inconspicuous fabric pull-tabs have been attached to the outer corners of the rectangle. To peel back the carpet when he wants to get at a hatch, the boatman simply takes hold of a tab and pulls.

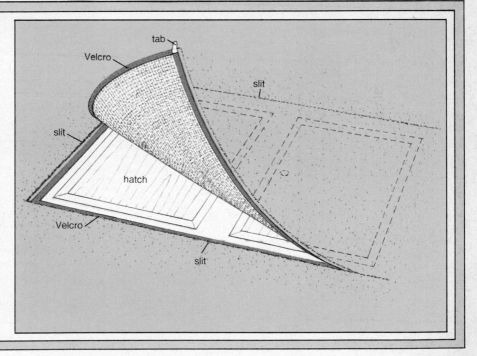

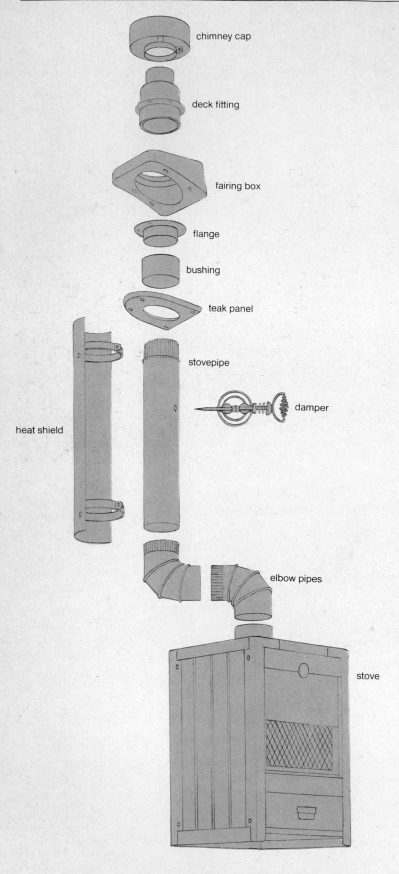

chimney cap

deck fitting

fairing box

flange

bushing

teak panel

stovepipe

heat shield

damper

elbow pipes

stove

An expanded drawing of the cabin stove installation described at right shows the stove and the fittings that form its venting system. The trickiest part of the installation involves the topmost sections of the system, between the teak masking panel and the pipe's cap, which sailors call a "Charley Noble" for some long-forgotten reason. These sections must fit snugly in and around a through-deck hole so the pipe's exit from the cabin is waterproof and fireproof.

A Stove for Cold Weather

The dry heat of a charcoal-burning cabin stove, like the 10-pound, 16-by-9-by-9-inch example shown on these pages, not only lengthens the comfortable cruising season, but also combats the plague of all cruising seasons: dampness below. But the benefits of warmth and dry air are accompanied by the perils of fire and acrid smoke, and a boatman must install the stove with the greatest care. For example, in a recessed area like the one on these pages, he must insulate the facing between the stove and the bulkhead on which it is mounted with asbestos and stainless-steel plates. Other surfaces within a foot of the stove's sides or four inches of its top or bottom must be similarly insulated. If the stovepipe is near a passageway or bulkhead, it should be insulated with a stainless-steel shield. The hole through the cabin top should also be lined with a stainless-steel bushing.

A suitable stove with proper accessories, shown at left, can be purchased through most major marine-supply houses. Two custom-made teak pieces were added to the assembly shown here: a fairing box to ensure a snug fit of the deck fitting on the cambered cabin top, and a decorative panel that covers the underside of the stovepipe's exit through the overhead. The construction of these extra pieces is explained overleaf.

Once the stove is installed and burning, the boatman should observe two rules: leave a port open to provide a draft and to keep the cabin clear of smoke and deadly carbon monoxide; never drape wet clothing over any part of the stove.

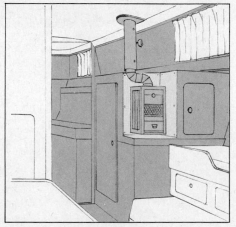

The best position for a stove is as close as possible to the center of the boat's belowdecks space. Usually, this is a spot forward in the main cabin; there the stove can be installed—with screws or, for extra security, with bolts—on any convenient bulkhead, such as the one shown here between the cabin and a hanging locker.

To create insulating panels for the mounting bulkhead and any nearby surfaces, first cut out paper templates to the proper sizes and configurations. Tape the template for the area behind the stove into position, and, while a helper hoists the stove into place, mark the location of the stove's bolt holes on the template (as shown). The protective plates—of 24-gauge stainless steel—can then be ordered from a metal shop, cut to size with bolt holes for the stove in their proper places, and with screw holes around the edges for fastening the plates to the surfaces to be insulated. Have the metalworker bevel the plates' outside corners and file all edges and corners smooth.

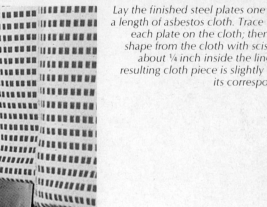

Lay the finished steel plates one at a time on a length of asbestos cloth. Trace the shape of each plate on the cloth; then cut out the shape from the cloth with scissors, staying about ¼ inch inside the line so that the resulting cloth piece is slightly smaller than its corresponding plate.

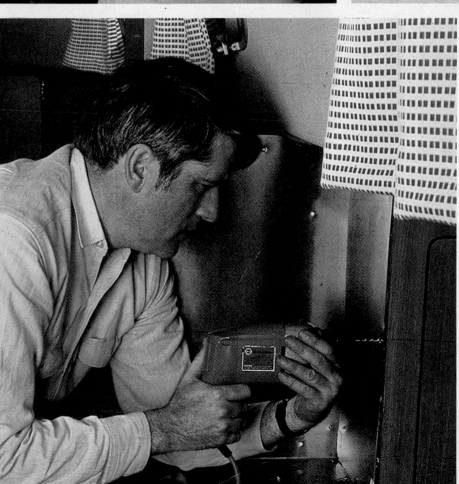

To mount the heat-insulating plates in the cabin, first tape each piece of asbestos to its corresponding piece of stainless steel. Starting with the bottom plate—if one is necessary—screw the sheets in position with stainless-steel screws. Remove the tape. To mount the stove, drill holes through the bulkhead using the predrilled holes in the metal sheets as guides. Fasten the stove in place with heavy-duty stainless-steel bolts or ¾-inch screws. Then connect the two pipe elbows and attach them to the stove.

To determine the center point of the stovepipe's exit hole through the overhead, hold the pipe alongside the upper edge of the top elbow joint and parallel to the position it will eventually occupy. Have a helper mark the overhead at the upper edge of the pipe (as shown at right and in the diagram below). Then draw a line equal to the radius of the pipe—in this case, 1½ inches—toward a point above the center of the opening in the elbow joint. The point can be double-checked by hanging a plumb line from the cabin top; the plumb should enter the center of the opening in the upper joint.

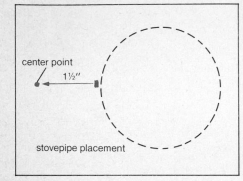

center point

1½″

stovepipe placement

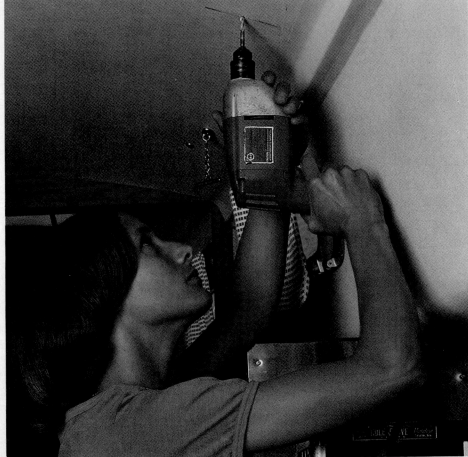

After marking the center of the stovepipe's exit hole as shown above, check topside to be sure that the hole will be well clear of any on-deck equipment. Return below, and holding an electric drill vertically—have your helper sight it from a distance—drill a pilot hole up through the deck.

Drill the exit hole in the top of the cabin with a four-inch hole saw, using the pilot hole as a guide and holding the drill vertically. First drill halfway through the deck from below. Complete the job from above decks, as shown, to keep the fiberglass from chipping. Now make the teak trim for the underside of the opening as follows: take an 8-by-7-by-½-inch piece of teak and fair it with sandpaper to fit against the cabin top. Have your helper hold it in position—at the edges for safety—while you drill it through from above with the hole saw. Shape and sand the edges of the piece; then set it aside.

To run the chimney through a sloped cabin top, make a teak fairing box, as shown below in cross section. Glue together two ⅞-inch teak pieces that are at least 1¾ inches wider and 3½ inches longer than the flange on the deck fitting. (For a severe slope, add extra wood.) Let the glued pieces set, then cut a five-inch hole through their center with a hole saw. Next, glue a ½-inch-thick piece of teak on top. When the glue dries, cut a three-inch hole for the chimney fitting. Mark a ½-inch taper on each side of the box, put it in a vise and saw along the lines with a handsaw. Round the edges by sanding.

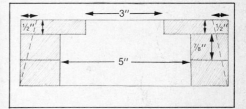

To fit the fairing box flush onto the curved cabin top, ask your helper to hold the box horizontally directly over the hole in the deck; check it with a level. Then, starting at an outboard corner, spread a pencil compass so its sharp steel point touches the cabin top, while its pencil makes a corresponding line on the side of the horizontally held box, as shown. Cut along this line with a saber saw. Sand the edges of the cut until the box and deck fit snugly together.

To complete the topside assembly, apply a generous amount of bedding compound around the hole on top of the fairing box. Slip the deck fitting through the top of the box so that its flange fits snugly against the box. Drill screw holes into the teak through the ready-drilled holes in the flange and screw the flange into place. Then apply bedding compound around the underside of the hole and slip the individual flange piece over the deck fitting and up against the fairing box as shown; screw the installation into place. Be sure that the screws through both flanges are set clear of each other.

To attach the topside assembly to the cabin top, mark spots for bolt holes ½ inch in from each corner of the top of the box. Set the box onto the deck so that the bottom of the chimney piece fits perfectly in the center of the vent hole in the deck. Drill holes through the box and the deck with a counterbore bit while a helper holds the box in position and drops bolts through each hole as it is completed to ensure an even fit.

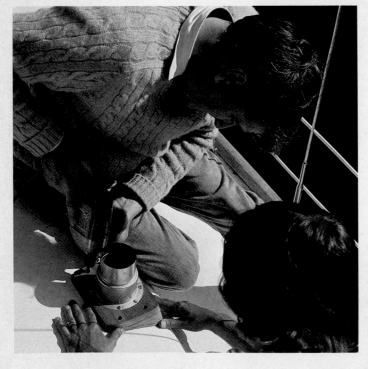

Remove the box and the bolts from the deck and slip the stainless-steel bushing into the deck hole so it rims the edges of the cabin top. Smooth a thick layer of bedding compound on the bottom of the fairing box, as shown at right; place it on the deck and bolt it down.

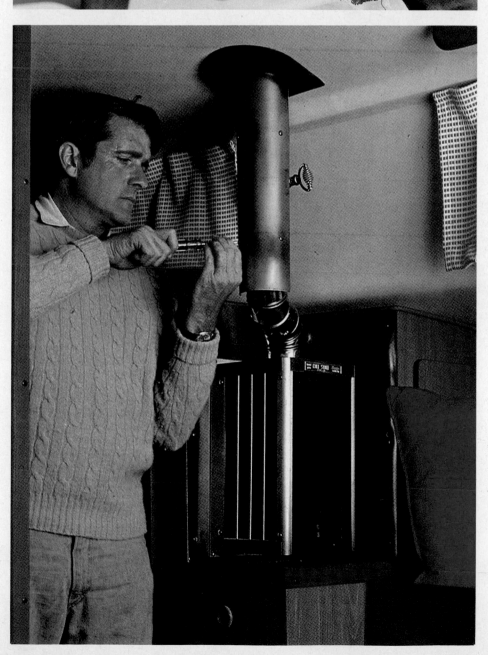

Fill the bolt holes on top of the fairing box with bungs dipped in resorcinol. Align the grain of the bungs with the grain of the fairing-box wood. Chisel or sand off any protruding stubs of the bungs and coat the top of each with glue to seal any cracks. Remove the excess. The chimney cap can then be fitted on, as shown, and excess bedding compound scraped off the cabin top with a razor blade.

Belowdecks, center the teak panel under the vent hole. Press it against the fairing-box bolts so that they leave impressions in the wood. Chisel out the impressions so the panel fits against the cabin top. Drill and screw the panel in place with ¾-inch screws. Bung the screw holes. Next slip the stovepipe into place, trimming the pipe, if necessary, with metal shears. Remove the pipe and drill two holes opposite each other at one end of the pipe for the damper. Insert the damper, replace the pipe and fasten it with a screw set through the pipe and elbow joint. Fasten the heat shield to the stovepipe.

This cabin in a cruising sloop shows off the results of belowdecks improvements put in by the owner. Cabin cushions have been re-covered with a heavy-duty marine fabric, and portholes have been curtained with bright polyester. A new charcoal-burning stove sits on the starboard counter (right, rear), and a teak tabletop with a drop-leaf extension holds the crew's dinner setting —including a potted geranium for a touch of dockside elegance.

A Choice of Timbers

Amid the constantly changing array of new materials used in and on modern boats—metal alloys, plastics, synthetic fibers —the uses of wood and of electric wire remain basically unaltered and of basic importance to the boatman. Though regular lumberyards may carry a smattering of boat lumber, specialized marine lumberyards generally offer a considerable assortment of seagoing timbers—which are usually stocked as unplaned one-inch-thick planks and in widths that are measured in ¼-inch increments. The rough lumber can be dressed at the yard to whatever dimension the boatman's particular project requires. The properties and the best uses of five woods especially suited to boat projects are listed below.

Wood	Characteristics and Handling	Uses
Teak	A fairly hard, yellowish tan wood that requires no finishing but should be cleaned periodically and treated with teak oil or sealant to prevent checking and staining and to preserve its color. Contains a natural oil that resists water and marine borers. Heavy, durable, low shrinkage. Dulls tools quickly.	Best for topside carpentry. Ideal for decks and handrails because of its slightly rough, nonskid surface. Beautiful and practical for below-decks decorative trim.
Mahogany	A rich red wood from Central America or Africa with a beautiful close grain that takes a lustrous finish. Resists fungi and insects, shrinks very little, but must be varnished or painted. Moderately soft and light with uniform consistency, holds fastenings reasonably well and cuts easily.	Excellent for both exterior and interior fittings. One of the finest woods for joiner work.
Philippine mahogany	A red wood resembling true mahoganies but with a coarse, uneven grain that is hard to plane smooth. Takes a good finish when sanded. Fairly decay resistant, but must be painted or varnished. Moderately soft, light and strong but splits easily and holds fastenings less well than true mahoganies.	Primarily suited for interior work that is not conspicuous.
White oak	A hard, strong wood that is easy to cut and shape. Superior in holding fastenings, bearing weight and resisting torque. Highly resistant to rot but will discolor if not varnished or painted.	Excellent for frames, for supporting heavy machinery or as a reinforcement—such as a corner support inside a deck locker.
Marine plywood	Durable, strong and unlikely to shrink or swell. Available in fir, teak, mahogany and other veneers. Should be cut with fine-toothed blades to avoid splintered edges, and planed obliquely and away from corners to prevent chipping. Seal edges with preservative against damp.	Versatile for use in above- and belowdecks fittings, lockers, bulkheads and doublers.

A Directory of Diameters

On boats, as elsewhere, electricity is measured in volts, watts and amperes, or amps. Voltage represents the intensity of the current in a circuit, amperage the amount of current, and wattage the rate at which current is consumed. Resistance in a wire carrying current to an appliance reduces the voltage delivered to the appliance. The longer the wire and the smaller its gauge, or diameter, the greater the voltage drop; excessive drop can drastically affect performance. A 10 per cent drop is tolerable for installations such as cabin lights, but for essentials, such as electronic equipment, the drop should not exceed 3 per cent. The tables below, based on American Boat and Yacht Council Safety Standards, show the minimum American Wire Gauge (A.W.G.) sizes for voltage drop limits at various wire lengths (source to load). The higher the gauge, the smaller the wire.

Recommended Wire-Gauge Sizes for 12-Volt, Two-Wire Systems

Length of wire to fixture in feet

Total current or amps* on circuit	10	15	20	25	30	35	40	45	50	55	60	
5	16	16	16	16	14	14	14	14	12	12	12	
10	16	14	14	12	12	12	10	10	10	10	8	**10% voltage drop wire gauges (A.W.G.)**
15	14	14	12	10	10	10	8	8	8	8	8	
20	14	12	10	8	8	8	6	6	6	6	6	
25	10	10	10	8	8	8	6	6	6	6	4	
5	14	12	12	10	10	8	8	8	8	8	6	
10	12	10	8	8	6	6	6	4	4	4	4	**3% voltage drop wire gauges (A.W.G.)**
15	10	8	6	6	4	4	4	4	2	2	2	
20	8	6	6	4	4	2	2	2	2	2	1	
25	8	6	4	4	2	2	2	1	1	1	0	

*To find amps when watts are known, divide watts by volts. For example, supplying three 40-watt bulbs from a 12-volt system requires a circuit capable of carrying 10 amps. To protect the wiring against an overload, install a fuse or circuit breaker rated at slightly fewer amps than the maximum the conductor can carry; any major appliance in the circuit usually has its own fuse.

Glossary

AC service box An electrical distribution center to which electrical current comes from shore power, and from which the AC current is dispensed on wires to switches and outlets throughout the boat. The service box contains either fuses or circuit breakers to guard against overloading the circuits.

Alternator A generator that produces alternating current. Aboard a boat, commonly used with a DC conversion device to charge the batteries.

Auxiliary switch In marine electricity, a safety device on a battery selector switch that prevents damage to the alternator when the selector switch is turned off.

Awl A pointed instrument used in marking surfaces or piercing small holes.

Backsaw A crosscut saw having a rectangular blade, a reinforced upper—or back—edge, and small teeth; used for joinery, usually in combination with a miter box.

Band saw A power saw with a long, continuous saw-toothed steel belt running over a pair of vertically opposed wheels; particularly adaptable for making curved cuts.

Basin wrench A plumbing tool whose toothed jaws are set at right angles to its shaft handle; used for tightening or removing nuts in hard-to-reach places, as under basins or sinks.

Bedding compound A viscous material, often based on silicones or epoxys, used as insulation to prevent seepage, especially between fittings and their mounting holes in a deck or hull.

Belt sander A power-driven device for sandpapering with a belt of sandpaper that rotates over two cylinders.

Bend To fasten, as a sail to the mast; to tie two lines together or to tie a line to an anchor; a knot by which an end of one line is tied to another to lengthen it.

Bias A direction that is diagonal to that of the threads in woven fabric. A true bias is at an angle of 45° to the weave of the fabric.

Bight An open loop in a line.

Bitter end The free end of a line.

Bonding A framework of conductors between metallic parts of a boat's structure that is used to neutralize errant electricity, thereby eliminating galvanic corrosion and radio interference—or even an explosion if a stray spark occurs near the carburetor or fuel-fill cap.

Braided line A line in which the strands are woven together, rather than twisted or laid up. Working lines are usually double braided, i.e., made up of two individually braided components, one inside for a core and a second outside for a cover.

Bridle A short length of extra-strong line made fast at either end to the towing eyes on a boat's transom, and used to hold the forward end of a water-ski towline clear of the towboat's engine; also, the portion of the towline, including the handle, held by the skier and leading to the after end of the main towline.

Bung A cylindrical plug of wood, much like a small cork, used to cover a countersunk screw or bolt.

Butt hinge A common household hinge, often used in cabinet work aboard a boat.

Bus bar A metal bar that serves as a common terminal point for positive or negative wires carrying current to and from lights and other accessories.

Bushing An electrically insulating lining used in a hole to protect wires passing through; also a cylindrical lining that protects or insulates the surface around an opening.

Cabin liner A sheath, usually made of fiberglass, that forms the innermost layer of the cabin.

Cabin sole The deck of the cabin.

Carpenter's compass A two-legged instrument with a point at the end of one of its legs and a pencil at the other end; used for drawing arcs.

Carpenter's square L-shaped metal ruler used for marking and checking square cuts, and for drawing vertical or parallel lines.

C clamp A C-shaped metal frame with an adjustable screw on one side used to hold pieces of work together for gluing, sawing or drilling.

Caulk To make seams watertight by filling them with a waterproof compound or other material.

Caulking gun A device used to caulk cracks and crevices. When the trigger is pulled, a ratchet inside the handle advances a notched plunger, pushing caulking through a nozzle in the front of the cartridge.

Cavitation The formation of a partial vacuum on or around the blades of a propeller, occurring whenever the propeller fails to get a solid bite in the water.

Cavitation plate A flat sheet of metal above a propeller designed to deflect downward the water discharged from the blades. This device gives the propeller a firmer bite in the water, increasing the motor's efficiency, and lessening the chance of cavitation.

Check valve A device, used in plumbing, that allows liquid to flow in only one direction.

Circular saw A heavy-duty power hand tool with interchangeable circular blades for sawing crosscuts, rips and bevels.

Coachwhipping A decorative covering made from line.

Companionway A passageway through which a ladder or flight of stairs leads from one deck level to another.

Counterbore bit A drill bit that in one operation bores a pilot, shank and countersink hole for a screw or bolt, so that the head can be set below the surface of the wood and covered with a bung or other filler.

Countersink bit A drill bit that widens the top of a screw hole into a V shape so that a flathead wood screw may be mounted flush or slightly below the surface.

Crown sennit A decorative device made by braiding the strands of a line in a series of crown knots, one superimposed upon the next.

Dado head A single, wide adjustable blade or multiple circular-saw blades used with a power saw to cut grooves or notches.

DC service box An electrical distribution

center; the place to which DC electrical current comes from the ship's battery, and from which the current is dispersed on wires to appliances throughout the boat. The service box contains either fuses or circuit breakers to guard against overloading the circuits.

Deck plate Small fitting set flush with the deck, forming the upper extremity of a piping system.

Dorade ventilator A deck box with a cowl and an internal arrangement that allows air but not water to enter the cabin.

Doubler A wood or metal plate bolted beneath a mounting surface for reinforcement.

Dowel A slender cylinder of solid wood; on boats, commonly used as a pin slipped through holes in abutting pieces to prevent slippage.

Doweling jig A metal device to guide a drill while making holes for dowels.

Elbow A piece of rigid piping bent at a 45° or 90° angle used for making sharp turns in a plumbing system; in heating stoves, a triple-jointed metal pipe that can be adjusted to many angles.

Electrician's snake A flexible wire tool used to guide electrical wiring from one place to another.

Electrolysis A term used loosely to describe galvanic corrosion caused by putting two different metals next to each other.

Engine grounding point A common terminal point on the engine block to which the negative battery terminal, the negative bus bar and the bonding system are connected.

Epoxy glue A resin-based adhesive of exceptional strength and durability, used in patching fiberglass or in joining materials.

Eye A loop in a line that has been seized, spliced or knotted.

Fid A tapered, pointed wooden or metal tool used for insertion between strands of line while splicing, sometimes having a hole in the blunt end for insertion of line; also, a length of bent wire used for splicing braided line.

Grab rail A securely mounted handhold on or below deck.

Hack saw A hand saw for cutting metals. The saw's steel frame adjusts to accept blades mounted between two lugs and is tensioned by means of a wing nut.

Half hitch A knot made by first passing the end of a line around an object or another line, then passing it around the standing part and bringing the end through the bight.

Hitch A method for securing a line to an object or to another line that is inert.

Hole saw A cylindrically shaped saw, with a drill bit in the center, that is fitted to a power drill for cutting holes.

Hose adapter A plumbing fitting used to connect a threaded pipe to a hose.

Hose clamp A stainless-steel band placed around an object to be clamped and drawn tight by means of a screw in the band-holding fixtures.

Jig A device used to maintain the correct positional relationship between a piece of work and a tool, or between parts of a project.

Knot Broadly, any intentional and firm interweaving of line or lines; specifically, a knot is formed when a line is turned back onto itself and tied, such as a bow line.

Laminate A surface composed of layers of bonded material; to create a single piece of material by building up bonded layers.

Lanyard A short, light line used for making fast such things as flags or the ends of stays; a rope handle for a knife, ditty bag, marlinespike, etc.

Lay The direction in which the strands of a line are twisted, usually right-handed or clockwise. In hard-laid line the strands are tightly twisted; in soft-laid line the strands are more nearly parallel.

Lock washer A small, incomplete circle of metal whose ends are not quite juxtaposed; inserted over a bolt and under a nut to prevent the nut from backing off when tightened.

Loop A bight of line that forms at least a

half circle. Bringing the end parts near each other forms a closed loop; leaving them apart makes an open one.

Machine bolt A heavy-duty fastener with a round, square, hex, button or countersunk head. Commonly used with two washers and a nut.

Marline Two-stranded nautical twine.

Marlinespike A pointed metal tool used in splicing.

Marry To unlay the ends of two lines and interlace the strands alternately, prior to splicing them.

Miter box A device for guiding a handsaw, usually a backsaw, at a specific angle for making joints in wood.

Monel A strong, rust-resistant metal alloy composed of approximately 67 per cent nickel, 28 per cent copper and 5 per cent iron and manganese; commonly used for fastenings, propellers and parts of metal instruments.

Noose A loop of line with a running knot.

Orbital sander A power-driven sandpapering device equipped with a rotating felt pad over which sandpaper has been mounted.

Overcast stitch A stitch that binds a fabric edge. It is made by drawing the needle through the fabric from the wrong side to the right side about ⅛ inch below the edge, then returning the needle to the wrong side—bringing it over the edge, not through the fabric—and then drawing it through from wrong to right side again.

Overhand knot A knot formed by making a loop in a line and feeding the bitter end back around the loop, in an over-and-under sequence. Used primarily as a building block in making other knots.

Piano hinge A narrow rectangular hinge with a small-diameter pin and numerous holes for screws; used for joining two edges that require support all along their lengths.

Pipe clamp Clamp made of a piece of pipe with one clamping arm fixed at one end and the other movable over the entire length of the pipe; especially useful for gluing together large projects.

Plug cutter A drill bit used to cut plugs —or bungs—of wood.

Protractor An instrument used for making and measuring angles.

Pylon A sturdy pole or tripod mounted on a water-ski boat to act as the on-board terminal for a towline.

Radial arm saw A heavy-duty circular power saw fixed to a movable arm and typically mounted above a sawing bench.

Resorcinol A waterproof synthetic resin used for gluing together absorptive surfaces such as wood.

Ring lug A connecting device that is crimped onto a wire end and then secured to a screw terminal.

Round turn Line brought completely around an object to form a closed loop.

Router A woodworking power tool with interchangeable revolving cutter bits for gouging out specified areas from the surface of a board. The tool adjusts vertically to control the depth of the cut.

Running stitch A basic hand stitch that is made by inserting a needle from the wrong side of the fabric and weaving the needle in and out of the fabric several times in evenly spaced stitches.

Saber saw A portable power saw with interchangeable blades, capable of crosscutting, ripping, sawing curves, and beveling.

Sail needle A heavy steel needle, triangular from point to midsection, then rounded to the eye; used in sailmaking.

Sailmaker's palm A stiff leather strap that fits around the hand and contains an inverted metal thimble; used to push a sailmaker's needle through heavy sailcloth.

Scupper A hole or opening in a rail, hatch or ventilator to allow water to drain off.

Sea cock A shutoff valve attached to through-hull fittings near or below the waterline.

Seize To bind two lines together or bind a line to another object.

Seizing wire All-purpose wire used to bind line together or to another object.

Selector switch A heavy-duty switch used to connect two batteries, separately or together, to the boat's electrical system.

Self-tapping screw A metal fastener that cuts its own hole threads as it is being inserted.

Selvage The lengthwise finished edge in woven fabric.

Serving A protective or decorative winding of tarred yarn, marline, or another similar material around a line.

Sister hooks A pair of hooks suspended from a common link and flat on their facing sides so that they lie together and form an eye when in use.

Skeg A fixed triangular fin extending down under the stern of a small boat and aiding the boat to follow a straight course.

Splice A method of joining together two ends of line or of creating a loop in a line by interweaving the strands.

Splice connector An insulated metal sleeve used to permanently fasten together two electrical wires by crimping the sleeve over one end of each.

Square knot A utility knot that is made of two overhand knots and used for binding together two ends of a line or joining two lines of equal size when the strain on either line is not great. Also called a reef knot.

Standing part The inactive part of a line, often near the midsection.

Starter solenoid A relay switch that connects the positive battery terminal to the engine starter motor when the start button is pressed.

Stopper knot Any knot used to prevent a line from running out through a block or fair-lead.

Stove bolt A metal fastener with a slotted round or flat head. Commonly used with two washers and a nut.

Table saw A circular power saw whose blade protrudes through a slot in a flat cutting surface, typically a table-like sawing bench.

Template A disposable pattern used as a guide to describe the outline of a project or a section of a project.

Transducer The sending-receiving device of a depth finder that transmits sonic pulses to the bottom, and then picks up the echoes.

Tuck In knot tying, to insert the end of a line between two other lines or between two parts of the same line. In splicing, to insert a strand between two other strands.

Twist bit A drill bit with spiral cutting grooves on its exterior to make clearance holes for bolts and screws.

Unlay To open up or separate the strands of a line.

Utility knife A general-purpose cutting tool with interchangeable steel blades.

V berths Twin bunks arranged in a V pattern, and typically placed in the forward part of the boat.

Vented loop Inverted U-shaped pipe with a vent at the top, used as a section in toilet discharge lines to prevent back siphoning.

Voltage regulator An electrical device that prevents the engine's alternator from overcharging or undercharging the battery.

Waterline The actual level of the water on a floating hull.

Welting Fabric-covered cording with exposed seam allowances that can be sewed into seams for decoration, and to reinforce the seams of furniture covers.

Whip To bind the end of a line with twine, cord or plastic sealant to prevent it from fraying.

Working end The fastened or manipulated end of a line.

Further Reading

General

Bramham, Ken, *Handyman Afloat and Ashore*. Adlard Coles Limited, 1972.

Brewer, Edward S., and Jim Betts, *Understanding Boat Design*. International Marine Publishing Company, 1971.

Cantin, Donald, *The Care and Maintenance of Small Boats*. Drake Publishers, Inc., 1973.

Chapelle, Howard I., *Boatbuilding*. W. W. Norton & Company, Inc., 1969.

Cobb, Boughton, Jr., *Fiberglass Boats, Construction and Maintenance*. Yachting Publishing Corporation, 1973.

De Kerchove, René, *International Maritime Dictionary*. D. Van Nostrand Company, Inc., 1961.

Duffet, John, *Modern Marine Maintenance*. Motor Boating & Sailing Books, 1973.

Henderson, Richard, with Bartlett S. Dunbar, *Sail and Power*. Naval Institute Press, 1973.

Herreshoff, L. Francis:
The Common Sense of Yacht Design. Caravan-Maritime Books, 1973.
Sensible Cruising Designs. International Marine Publishing Company, 1973.

Kenealy, James P., *Boating from Bow to Stern*. Hawthorn Books, Inc., 1966.

Kinney, Francis S., *Skene's Elements of Yacht Design*. Dodd, Mead & Company, 1962.

Motor Craft. National Fire Protection Association, 1972.

Nicholson, Ian, *Surveying Small Craft*. International Marine Publishing Company, 1974.

Safety Standards for Small Craft. American Boat and Yacht Council Inc., 1973-1974.

Shrager, Arthur N., *Elementary Metallurgy and Metallography*. Dover Publications Inc., 1961.

Steward, Robert M., *Boatbuilding Manual*. International Marine Publishing Company, 1970.

Street, Donald M., Jr., *The Ocean Sailing Yacht*. W. W. Norton & Company, Inc., 1973.

Toghill, Jeff, *Boat Owner's Maintenance Manual*. John de Graff, Inc., 1970.

Verney, Michael:
Boat Maintenance by the Amateur. Winchester Press, 1970.
Boat Repairs and Conversions. International Marine Publishing Company, 1974.

Weeks, Morris, Jr., ed., *The Complete Boating Encyclopedia*. Golden Press, 1964.

Willis, Melvin D. C., *Boatbuilding and Repairing with Fiberglass*. International Marine Publishing Company, 1972.

Zadig, Ernest A.:
The Boatman's Guide to Modern Marine Materials. Motor Boating & Sailing Books, 1974.
The Complete Book of Boating. Prentice-Hall, 1972.

Carpentry

Capotosto, Rosario, *Complete Book of Woodworking*. Book Division, Times Mirror Magazines, Inc., 1975.

Groneman, Chris H., *General Woodworking*. McGraw-Hill Company, 1971.

Schuler, Stanley, *The Illustrated Encyclopedia of Carpentry & Woodworking Tools, Terms & Materials*. Pequot Press/Random House, 1973.

Smith, Hervey Garrett, *Boat Carpentry*. Van Nostrand Reinhold Company, 1965.

Engines and Electrical Systems

French, John, *Electrical and Electronic Equipment for Yachts*. Dodd, Mead & Company, 1974.

Kahan, Del F., *Marine Electrical Practice Pleasure Craft Direct Current Systems*. Marinetics Press, 1975.

Miller, Conrad:
Small Boat Engines Inboard and Outboard. Sheridan House, 1970.
Your Boat's Electrical System. The Hearst Corporation, 1972.

The Radio Amateur's Handbook. The American Radio Relay League Inc., 1973.

Sands, Leo G., *Marine Electronics Handbook*. Tab Books, 1973.

United States Power Squadrons, *Marine Engines and Equipment*. Educational Department, U.S. Power Squadrons, 1972.

West, Jack, *Modern Powerboats*. Van Nostrand Reinhold Company, 1970.

Witt, Glen L., *Inboard Motor Installations in Small Boats*. Glenn, 1960.

Ropework

Ashley, Clifford W., *The Ashley Book of Knots*. Doubleday & Company, Inc., 1944.

Day, Cyrus Lawrence, *The Art of Knotting and Splicing*. Naval Institute Press, 1970.

Graumont, Raoul, and John Hensel, *Encyclopedia of Knots and Fancy Rope Work*. Cornell Maritime Press, Inc., 1952.

Smith, Hervey Garrett, *The Marlinspike Sailor*. John de Graff, Inc., 1971.

Snyder, Paul and Arthur, *Knots & Lines Illustrated*. John de Graff, Inc., 1967.

Marine-Supply Catalogues

Accessories for Power & Sailboats, H & L Marine Woodwork Inc., 2323 West 190th St., Redondo Beach, California 90278.

James Bliss & Co., Inc., *Everything Marine*, Route 128, Dedham, Massachusetts 02026.

Buck-Algonquin Marine Hardware, Second Street and Columbia Avenue, Philadelphia, Pennsylvania 19122.

Defender Industries, Inc., *Marine Buyers' Guide*, 255 Main Street, New Rochelle, New York 10801.

East End Supply Co., Inc., 203 Front Street, Greenport, New York 11944.

Goldbergs' Marine, 202 Market Street, Philadelphia, Pennsylvania 19106 or 3 West 46th Street, New York, New York 10036.

Klest Products Corp., P.O. Box 707, East Boston, Massachusetts 02128.

Lands End Yachtsman's Equipment Guide, 2241 North Elston Avenue, Chicago, Illinois 60611.

Manhattan Marine, 116 Chambers Street, New York, New York 10007.

Marine Catalog, Jabsco Products ITT, 1485 Dale Way, Costa Mesa, California 92626.

The Mariner's Catalog, International Marine Publishing Co., Camden, Maine 04843.

Mast Abeam, 1186 Dalon Rd., N.E., Atlanta, Georgia 30306.

Merriman Holbrook, Grand River, Ohio 44045 or 1791 Reynolds Avenue, Irvine, California 92705.

Nicro Fico, 2065 West Avenue 140th, San Leandro, California 94577.

Schaefer Marine Products, Industrial Park, New Bedford, Massachusetts 02745.

The Ship's Log, Wilcox-Crittenden, Middletown, Connecticut 06457.

Spyglass, 2415 Webster Street, Alameda, California 94501.

Acknowledgments

For their help on this volume, the editors are especially indebted to: Gil Cigal, electrical consultant, Brooklyn, New York; Tom Crowley, ropework consultant, The Rope Gallery, New York City; Gretel Courtney, sewing consultant, New York City; David A. Hassell, carpentry consultant, The Wooden World, Bellport, New York; Stanley Postek, ropework consultant, The Rope Gallery, New York City; and Art Van Sciver, electrical consultant, Darien, Connecticut.

The index was prepared by Anita R. Beckerman. The editors also thank: Robert E. Armbruster, Griffith Marine Navigation Inc., New Rochelle, New York; Bertram Yacht, Miami, Florida; James T. Chapman, Griffith Marine Navigation Inc., New Rochelle, New York; Gordon Crowell, Raritan Engineering Company, Millville, New Jersey; Edwin L. Deveau, Kretzer Boatworks, City Island, New York; Jack Dillon, Byram, Connecticut; Tyson Dominy, Jr., Bellport, New York; Robert M. Doty, Bomar Inc., Westport, Connecticut; E. I. Du Pont de Nemours & Company, Wilmington, Delaware; John Ellsworth, Pearson Yachts, Portsmouth, Rhode Island; R. Grosvenor Ely, Boatworks Inc., Rowayton, Connecticut; Richard E. Emery, Griffith Marine Navigation Inc., New Rochelle, New York; Kenneth Garelick, Garelick Mfg. Co., St. Paul Park, Minnesota; The Guest Corporation, West Hartford, Connecticut; William Hart, Connecticut Marine Electronics Inc., Rowayton, Connecticut; Jack Herscovitz, Aqualarm Inc., Gardena, California; Jackie Hubbard, Stamford, Connecticut; Patricia Hassell, Bellport, New York; Hercules Incorporated, Wilmington, Delaware; Del F. Kahan, Marinetics Corporation, Newport Beach, California; Mr. and Mrs. Justin E. Kerwin, Weston, Massachusetts; Kirsch Company, New York; William Lince, Ratelco Inc., Seattle, Washington; G. James Lippmann, American Boat & Yacht Council, Inc., New York City; Manhattan Marine, New York City; James L. Martin, Mar-Lou Draperies, Fall River, Massachusetts; David G. Marvin, New Canaan, Connecticut; Nib Massa, Coast Cushion Co. Inc., Warren, Rhode Island; David Newton, Maidstone Shipyard, Easthampton, New York; Jeffrey Page, Boatworks, Inc., Rowayton, Connecticut; Chet Phetteplace, Bacharach Instrument Company, Mountain View, California; Robert Pierce, O'Day, A Bangor Punta Company, Fall River, Massachusetts; Cpt. Al Pilvinis, Great Neck, New York; Robert Preston, Johnson Outboards, Waukegan, Illinois; Pro-Line Manufacturing, Milwaukee, Wisconsin; Terri Rassmusen, Glen Rock, New Jersey; Richard Rieder, New York City; Rockland Industries Inc., Brooklandville, Maryland; Robert Schroer, Evinrude Motors, Milwaukee, Wisconsin; Don Schultz, Rowayton, Connecticut; Joseph J. Sencen Jr., Kirsch Company, New York City; Ronald S. Tebutt, Saltair Shinnecock, Inc., Hampton Bays, New York; Sam Thomas, Raritan Engineering Company, Millville, New Jersey; Robert N. Turner Jr., Sudbury Laboratory, Inc., Sudbury, Massachusetts; Uniroyal Inc., New York City; Ve-Ve Incorporated, Anoka, Minnesota; Preston Waterman, Bellport, New York; Ed Winarski, Pearson Yachts, Portsmouth, Rhode Island; John Wisner, Boatworks Inc., Rowayton, Connecticut; Raymond Yturraspe, Griffith Marine Inc., New Rochelle, New York; Walter Zielenski, Bellport, New York.

Picture Credits

Index
Numerals in italics indicate a photograph or drawing of the subject mentioned.